EVERLASTING LIGHT

A Journey from Promise to Presence

An Advent Devotional by Carlos A. Zazueta
with Charles R. Swindoll

INSIGHT FOR LIVING

The Bible-Teaching Ministry of Pastor Charles R. Swindoll

EVERLASTING LIGHT

A Journey from Promise to Presence

by Carlos A. Zazueta
with Charles R. Swindoll

ACKNOWLEDGMENTS

President, Insight for Living: Charissa Swindoll Gaither

Senior Vice President, Communications and Engagement: Linda Ricks, BBA, Marketing and Accounting, Baylor University

Senior Vice President, *Searching the Scriptures* Ministries: Aaron Massey, ThM, Dallas Theological Seminary

Vice President, *Searching the Scriptures* Ministries: Bryce Klabunde, ThM, Dallas Theological Seminary; DMin, Western Seminary

Substantive Editor: Jim Craft, MA, English, Mississippi College; MA, Christian Studies, Dallas Theological Seminary

Print Communications Manager, Publishing: Autumn Swindoll, BA, Humanities, Biola University

Production Editor: Katie Hayes, BA, Communications, Southwest Baptist University

Graphic Designer: Laura Dubroc, BFA, Advertising Design, University of Louisiana at Lafayette

Production Artist: Nancy Gustine, BFA, Advertising Art, University of North Texas

Cover Image: fotoyou | Adobestock.com

ISBN: 978-1-62655-249-4

DEDICATION

To Christ

the Sun that never sets,

the promise that pierced the shadows,

the radiance that shattered the night

and became for us our Everlasting Light.

To Karla

whose life reflects that Light with steady tenderness,

and whose presence has been to me

like a lamp glowing warmly in our home.

To Asher

our little flickering flame,

whose playful, tireless brightness

reminds us each day

that the Light still shines among us.

CONTENTS

A PASTORAL NOTE

Dear reader and fellow traveler,

Few things stir the heart like the promise of light after a long night. We know that feeling of gloom when it seems the night will never end—when uncertainty lingers, when waiting weighs heavy, when life dims. Advent answers that ache. It is more than tradition; it is a sacred invitation to let hope rekindle and to watch darkness give way to daybreak.

This devotional is a lantern—not to dazzle but to guide. Page by page, you'll trace a steady dawn from the first glimmer of hope to the full radiance of Christ's presence. Jesus did not come merely to brighten a manger. He came to set our hearts ablaze with hope, peace, joy, and enduring love—and His light still shines today, even in our darkest hours.

For nearly two decades, I have served alongside Pastor Charles R. Swindoll as pastor overseeing the Spanish-language ministries at Stonebriar Community Church and at Insight for Living as Chuck's "voice" in Spanish on the radio program, *Visión Para Vivir*, the Spanish-language version of *Insight for Living*.

Pastor Chuck is a man whose love for Scripture and for our Savior has profoundly influenced my life and my ministry. You will sense his pastoral wisdom in these pages. I am grateful for his friendship—and grateful to walk this path with you.

How should you read this book? Read unhurried. Open the Word, whisper a prayer, welcome Christ's presence, and then take one step of obedience into your day. Let Jesus, the Light, move you from page to practice—in conversations, choices, and acts of quiet courage.

This is your charge as you begin: Read with expectation. Rise with intention. Go with the glow of Christ within you.

With affection and gratitude,

Carlos A. Zazueta

Carlos A. Zazueta
Fellow pilgrim of the Light

INTRODUCTION

As the nights grow long and the days grow brief, something in us aches for more than lamps that brighten a room. We long for a radiance that warms the heart and rekindles hope. Advent meets us in this longing. It invites us to pause, breathe deeply, and remember: even in our darkest seasons, Jesus, the Light, has come—and still shines.

Though Advent closes the calendar year, it also opens the Christian liturgical year and sets us at the beginning of redemption's story. This is more than a countdown to Christmas; it is a season that reorients our hearts to Christ: the Child of Bethlehem who came, the Savior who comes to us now, and the King who will come again in glory.

For centuries, believers have embraced Advent as a time of waiting, reflection, and repentance. Meanwhile, our culture rushes forward in a flurry of noise and activity: endless lists, crowded calendars, last-minute greeting cards, school concerts, and sugar-dusted kitchens. At times, the cheerful voices of carolers or a children's Christmas pageant brings smiles to our faces. Yet even these treasured moments can be swallowed by the hurry. Advent calls us to something different: a quiet space, a slower pace, a waiting filled with hope.

The word *Advent* comes from the Latin *adventus*, meaning "coming." It celebrates both Christ's first coming in Bethlehem and His promised return. We live in that sacred tension of "already and not yet." Christ has come, and yet we still await His appearing. Advent gives us holy permission to both grieve and rejoice—to bring our longings before God while holding fast to the hope that cannot fail.

At the heart of this season lies the *Cycle of Light*—a symbolic journey through five themes: **Hope**, **Peace**, **Joy**, **Love**, and **Arrival**. Many churches begin Sundays before Christmas with an Advent wreath, lighting one candle each week: Hope, Peace, Joy, and Love, until the final Christ candle shines on Christmas. The brightness grows week by week, like dawn breaking on the horizon—quiet, steady, and sure.

This is why our *Cycle of Light* moves like discipleship itself—hope teaches us to wait, peace trains us to rest in His nearness, joy strengthens us to endure, love sends us toward others, and the arrival crowns it all with Christ's presence.

A few Christmases ago, I saw this truth reflected in my son Asher's eyes. While decorating our home, I noticed a small but meaningful connection between us: we both love Christmas lights. Their warm glow does more than brighten a room—it stirs the heart with wonder. As we unpacked decorations, I found an old Charlie Brown Christmas tree I once kept in my office—a single drooping branch with one red ornament—and set it in his room. He studied it for a moment and asked, "But Papi, where are the lights? If it doesn't have lights, it's not a Christmas tree."

I smiled, ready to correct him, but stopped. In his innocent wisdom, he was right. Without the Light, it isn't Christmas. Without Christ, Christmas loses its meaning.

The prophet Isaiah wrote,

> *"No longer will you need the sun to shine by day,*
> *nor the moon to give its light by night,*
> *for the LORD your God will be your everlasting light*
> *and your God will be your glory."* (Isaiah 60:19)

John echoed the same truth: *"The one who is the true light, who gives light to everyone, was coming into the world"* (John 1:9). This is Advent's heartbeat: Christ, our Everlasting Light shines from prophecy to manger, through His people today, and into eternity.

This devotional is a small lantern for that journey. It will guide you through Advent's *Cycle of Light*—Hope that pierces the night, Peace that steadies our steps, Joy that brightens the heart, Love that warms the soul, and the Arrival that fills the world with Christ's brilliance. To deepen the experience, you may wish to keep a nativity set or an Advent wreath nearby as you read.

Each daily devotional includes:

- A Scripture passage to anchor your heart
- A quote from Pastor Chuck Swindoll to shape your thinking
- A devotional reflection to draw you toward the Light
- A prayer and a simple practice to guide your day

The purpose of these pages is to help you embody the hope you profess, carry the peace you've received, and shine with the joy and love of Christ where you live, work, and worship. Advent is not a sentiment to admire but a light to bear. As you read, ask the Spirit to kindle Christ's life within you—so that His light does more than illumine your path; it becomes a lamp for others.

This is the journey of Advent: a growing light within, until Christ fills every shadow with His glory.

EVERLASTING
LIGHT

A Journey from Promise to Presence

HOPE

THE GLIMMER
OF **HOPE**

The Light That Pierces the Deepest Night
{ December 1–5 }

What do we cling to when God seems quiet and the future feels uncertain?

Advent begins here—with a first glimmer of hope. Between the final words of the prophet Malachi and the birth of Christ in Bethlehem, four centuries passed without a prophetic voice or divine revelation. It was a long silence, but not a divine absence. Beneath the stillness, God was preparing the way: languages spread, roads were laid, empires shifted. When the time was right, the Promised One stepped into history. Hope was already at work before dawn broke.

Hope is the first candle of Advent. It does not expose every detail; it assures us that daybreak is on the horizon. The prophets held this lamp high—Isaiah spoke of a great light for those who walk in darkness; Micah pointed to a ruler from Bethlehem; Numbers foretold a star that would rise. These words became kindling for a weary people, and for us. We start this week with the same posture: trusting the God who keeps His Word.

I remember a season when my wife Karla and I sensed God leading us away from a ministry we loved in Central Texas. No job offer arrived, no map appeared, no clear path emerged. Only the ache of surrender and the silence that followed our yes. Still, we began packing, not because we had answers but because we held to God's promise: *"I will never leave you"* (Hebrews 13:5 ESV). That promise became our anchor. Hope became a daily choice—quiet prayers, a worn Bible, boxes labeled in faith.

> **Hope does not pretend the night is bright. It endures the night because it knows the sun will rise.**

In time, doors opened, guidance came, and provision followed. We learned that *hope is not the absence of fear; it is the presence of trust in a faithful Guide.*

Scripture describes "hope" with the Hebrew words *yakhal*, "waiting patiently" and *qavah*, "waiting with tension and expectation." Hope does not pretend the night is bright. It endures the night because it knows the sun will rise.

Consider the travelers from the East. When they saw a new star, they didn't merely admire it. They moved toward it. Guided by ancient prophecies—perhaps Daniel's witness in Babylon—they recalled:

> *A star will rise from Jacob;*
> *a scepter will emerge from Israel.* (Numbers 24:17)

Hope carried them first to Jerusalem and then to Bethlehem. When the star led them to the place where Jesus was, *"they were filled with joy!"* (Matthew 2:10). Entering the house, they saw the child and bowed down to worship Him.

Their journey teaches us that true hope is active. It moves us to seek, to follow, and to worship. It lifts our gaze, trains us to wait with expectation, and draws us to walk by the Light through every shadow until the day hope is fully fulfilled and "every knee will bow" and "every tongue will confess that Jesus Christ is Lord" (Philippians 2:10–11 NASB).

This Advent, let hope lead you. Not a fragile hope that collapses under disappointment but a steadfast hope rooted in the promises of God, who always prepares the way, even when we cannot yet see it.

> *I am counting on the LORD;*
> *yes, I am counting on him.*
> *I have put my hope in his word.* (Psalm 130:5)

And when hope has steadied your gaze, you are ready for the next candle: peace. If hope teaches us to wait for dawn, peace is the Light's posture within us—resting in God's nearness even while the night is long.

———————————————————————

Advent Wreath: Prophecy Candle (Purple)

Symbolizes the hope and anticipation of Christ's coming, as foretold by the prophets

Nativity Action: Set up the stable.

Scripture Reading: Isaiah 9:2–6

Reflection: As you light the first candle, ask: *Where do I need God's Light to pierce the darkness in my life?* Let hope rise as you wait on His promises.

December 1

HOLD TIGHT TO YOUR HOPE

*Let us hold tightly without wavering
to the hope we affirm,
for God can be trusted to keep his promise.*

HEBREWS 10:23

Hope is not a finger-crossing, wishful kind of thinking. It is a confident expectation that rests in God—who is faithful and always keeps His word. With your past justification as your footing and your future hope as your fuel, you can take the present journey through trials without losing your joy and peace. That's not wishful thinking. That's unquenchable hope.

— **Charles R. Swindoll**

Reflection

We often misunderstand hope, imagining it as a fragile wish tossed up to the heavens with fingers crossed, eyes shut, longing for the best. But biblical hope is not like that. It's steady and sure, a confident trust in God's character and His promises.

When we lit the first candle of Advent, we saw a flicker in the dark; today, that flame grows steadier. Hope doesn't remove hardship; it gives us courage to face it, knowing God is with us in the midst of it.

The writer of Hebrews urged weary believers living far from comfort and on the verge of quitting, *"Hold tightly to your hope."* Their confidence rested in God's faithfulness rather than their own strength.

Hope in Christ doesn't sit idly, waiting for things to improve; it leans forward. It says, *"I don't know how this ends, but I trust the One who does."* That posture sustains us in the tension between "already" and "not yet." Christ has come, yet we still groan under the weight of a broken world. We see it in the headlines, on our social media feeds, in our homes, and within our hearts.

Some days, hope feels like a stretch. Yet Advent doesn't ask us to deny the pain; it calls us to drop our anchor of faith deeper. We don't cling to hope with white-knuckled fists; we rest in the hands of the One who holds us.

This isn't fragile hope. It's the same resilient hope that carried the early church through loss and persecution. They endured through pain because Jesus had come, and they knew He would come again. And He will.

So if today feels shaky, pause and breathe. Remember: *"God can be trusted to keep his promise"* (Hebrews 10:23). You don't need to muster your own strength. Lean on His. Even on the longest night, the candle of hope still burns. Hope is not the absence of pain; it is the decision to trust in the dark what God revealed in the light.

The waiting may be long and the silence heavy, but take heart: God is never idle. He is still God. Sometimes, He allows the chaos to teach us lessons that comfort never could.

The Light is coming. Until He appears, He's still writing your story with grace and truth. Hold tight to your hope—lift it like a lamp—and take the next faithful step.

Prayer

Lord, thank You for being the anchor of my hope. When I feel weak, help me cling to Your promises. Teach me to trust Your timing and walk each day with confidence that You are near. Let hope shape how I love, lead, and live. Amen.

Advent Application

What promise can you cling to today? One to hold might be this:

> *And we know that in all things God works for the good of those who love him, who have been called according to his purpose.* (Romans 8:28 NIV)

How could sharing this truth encourage someone who's struggling? Speak it, live it, and remind him or her that they are not alone. Take one step today: send a text, make a call, or pray with someone who needs hope.

December 2

ANTICIPATE GOD'S FRESH MERCIES

The faithful love of the LORD never ends!
His mercies never cease.
Great is his faithfulness;
his mercies begin afresh each morning.

LAMENTATIONS 3:22–23

The people who have grown deep in their relationship with God have learned to wait with anticipation instead of worry. They know that God keeps His promises, so they don't fret over whether the fulfillment will come but only when it will take place. For us, within the flow of time, waiting often feels like an eternity. Everybody I know is waiting for something—waiting for relief, an answer to prayer, a dream to be fulfilled.

— Charles R. Swindoll

Reflection

Today, the candle of hope glows more steadily; its flame burns brighter—fueled by a deeper trust in the One who greets us each morning with new mercies.

We're all waiting for something: healing, direction, peace, a long-closed door to open, or a heavy burden to lift. In a culture that prizes instant results, waiting can feel like failure. Yet in God's kingdom, waiting is never wasted. It becomes sacred ground where love deepens, faith matures, and hope quietly takes root. Waiting may be quiet, but it is never empty. In the stillness, God's mercy often arrives so gently we almost miss it.

Throughout Scripture, light stands as a symbol of both creation and redemption—at the dawn of creation, when God said, *"Let there be light"* (Genesis 1:3) and at the arrival of Jesus, the Light of the World. Like mercy, that light rarely explodes all at once. It rises slowly, the way dawn filters into a shadowed room. If you're waiting for healing, clarity, or a fresh beginning, take refuge in God. What feels like a delay might be His way of clearing the path ahead.

I know this firsthand. For years I longed to be married and start a family. Yet as I followed God's call into full-time ministry, that hope seemed to fade. The waiting stretched longer than I had imagined, and I began to wonder if that door had closed forever.

Then, in God's perfect timing, my desire was fulfilled—unexpectedly, in Israel. I was serving as a bus shepherd during an Insight for Living tour of the Holy Land. Before the trip, a friend smiled and said, *"You never know—you might meet someone special."* I brushed it off politely.

One quiet morning on the Sea of Galilee, Pastor Chuck Swindoll invited us to cast a symbolic burden into the water. I chose a small stone to represent my singleness—and my longing for companionship—and I released it to God in prayer.

That very afternoon, I sat beside a young woman I had noticed on the bus but never met. We began to talk. To our surprise, we attended the same church at different service times. Friendship grew into a relationship. And in time, Pastor Chuck officiated our wedding—two lives, two languages, one God. His mercy met me there, in His time.

Waiting rarely feels easy, but it is never time wasted. Often, it is in the quiet where God does His deepest work. Trust that His mercy is already rising, even if you cannot yet see the light. Advent is not breath held tight until something changes; it is deep breathing in His promises and steady walking by their glow.

Today the candle of hope burns brighter, not because a circumstance has shifted our mind-set but because our trust has grown deeper. His love holds, His mercies endure, and His light—though it rises slowly—always comes.

Lift your lamp and step forward—the God whose mercies meet the morning is already meeting you today.

Prayer

Father, thank You for Your mercy that renews each morning. Help me wait with trust, not fear. Teach me to expect Your goodness, even when answers are slow. Let Your presence be the steady light that guides me today. In Jesus' name, amen.

Advent Application

Are you in a period of waiting? If so, write it down. Identify one mercy you've already received this morning—however small—and thank God for it.

December 3

FOLLOW THE LIGHT OF GOD'S PROMISES

*Your word is a lamp to guide my feet
and a light for my path.*

PSALM 119:105

God's Book is a veritable storehouse of promises—over seven thousand of them. They are verbal guarantees in writing, signed by the Creator Himself. But let's be wise: not every promise is ours to claim. Some are historical, others conditional. Even so, many are meant for us today. So take your stand, not outside the premises but firmly on the promises. In the darkness, God's Word doesn't just inform us—it guides us, step by step, one promise at a time.

— Charles R. Swindoll

Reflection

The Advent candle now burns with a steady flame. What began as a fragile flicker has become a guiding light. We have clung to hope and learned to wait with expectation. Now, we are called to follow, to take the next step by the light of God's promises, even when the path ahead is dim or hidden.

God's Word is not a floodlight exposing the path to the horizon; it is a lantern—small, yet sufficient—showing just the next step. As Psalm 119:105 reminds us, *"Your word is a lamp to guide my feet and a light for my path."* It may not offer full clarity, but it always provides what we need for today. This is the heart of biblical hope: trusting God one promise at a time.

We crave certainty. We want to know how the story ends, when prayers will be answered, why waiting lingers. God rarely hands us the entire picture. Instead, He gives us Himself and His Word, and that is more than enough. His promises outlast our appetite for predictability, our need to know what's next. They anchor us in what will not shake.

The prophets knew this truth. They walked through darkness, proclaiming what they would not live to see, yet they trusted and followed. They declared with unwavering conviction: *The Light is coming.* Their assurance rested not in outcomes but in the One who had spoken.

We stand in that same line of faith. Scripture does not sell quick fixes; it offers free enduring truth for unsettled days. Some promises were bound to a specific moment in history; many still speak directly to our hearts—relevant, reliable, and radiant with hope. Yet these promises only guide us when we engage with them.

Open the Word. Read not merely for information but for direction. Ask God to show you the next step—not the next five years but the next faithful choice. Whether you're facing a major decision or simply carrying a weary heart, remember this: *God may not remove every shadow, but He will be the light within it.*

Sometimes, the lamp is carried in another's hand. Decades ago, a couple named Sandi and Gary visited our church in Culiacán, Mexico, on a short-term mission trip. They brought a shoebox filled with cassette tapes and a book by Pastor Chuck Swindoll. But what impressed me most was not what they gave but how they lived.

With humility and love, they encouraged me to consider studying at Dallas Theological Seminary. Their quiet confidence in me became a turning point. They did more than speak truth—they *embodied* it. They became spiritual parents, not from obligation but from a deep love for God's mission and a willingness to invest in a young man who could not yet see his own potential.

Through their encouragement, I learned to approach Scripture with confidence and humility, to trust its promises and to teach its truths. They showed me that God's light often shines through ordinary obedience: people who speak life, who show up, and who believe in others long before others believe in themselves.

Often the next step is revealed by the steady glow of someone else's faithfulness.

Lift the lamp of His Word, take the next faithful step, and become the light someone else needs to see.

Prayer

Lord, thank You for Your Word that lights my path. When I can't see what's ahead, help me trust the promises You've already spoken. Lead me with Your truth and teach me to walk in faith, one step at a time. Amen.

Advent Application

Thank God today for someone who has been a guiding light in your faith journey, and—if possible—tell him or her. Ask God who He is inviting you to encourage and guide right now.

December 4

ANCHOR YOURSELF IN GOD'S TIMING

Let all that I am wait quietly before God,
for my hope is in him.

PSALM 62:5

When God prepares us for effective ministry, He often includes what we would rather omit—a season of waiting. In that waiting, He cultivates patience, humility, and depth. He reminds us that we are not the star attraction. And when the time is right—His time, not ours—He uses us in ways we never expected. Waiting quietly before Him isn't wasted time. It's anchoring time. It's the place where hope grows deep.

— Charles R. Swindoll

Reflection

At this point in our journey, the light of Advent burns with quiet strength. What began as a glimmer of hope has deepened into something steady and sure. Today, we're invited to let that light anchor us—to trust God's perfect timing rather than chase quick answers.

Waiting is one of the hardest disciplines of faith. Our culture trains us for speed—instant messages, overnight deliveries, same-day solutions. So, when God calls us to wait, we often assume something must be wrong. Yet Advent tells a different story. It tells us that waiting is not a punishment—it's preparation. It's not the absence of God's work; it's the sacred space where He often begins His deepest work.

Psalm 62:5 is both poetic and practical: *"Let all that I am wait quietly before God."* Not anxiously, not frantically but quietly, with trust. David wrote those words from a place of conflict rather than comfort. His hope was not in better circumstances—it was in God Himself.

Recently, our son Asher began asking us for something simple yet important to him: to download a particular game app. Most of his classmates already had it, and he longed to join their games and conversations. We told him he would need to wait until his ninth birthday. And so, he's been waiting—but not passively. Every few nights, he whispers the request in prayer. Not with frustration, but with hope. He has even circled the date on his calendar.

One evening, after praying quietly, he said, *"I think God is getting everything ready."* That line stopped me. He wasn't discouraged by the wait. He was trusting—fully, quietly—like a child who knows his father loves him and gives what is best at the right time.

That day, my eight-year-old taught me more about waiting than many sermons have. He reminded me that waiting is more than enduring silence; it is choosing to trust the One who holds time in His hands. Not as a servant dreading delay, but as a beloved child resting in the Father's goodness.

God never wastes the waiting. He uses it to deepen us, to slow us enough to hear His voice, to remind us that we're not the center of the story—though we are lovingly held within it. Often, the clearest moments come when we pause long enough to receive His peace without demanding answers. The waiting becomes holy ground where patience takes root.

So today, resist the urge to rush ahead. Anchor yourself in His presence. Trust that God's timing is never wrong. In the waiting, He is at work around you and within you.

As the Advent light grows stronger, remember: hope carries you as you carry its light.

Prayer

God, teach me to wait well. Quiet my anxious thoughts and anchor my heart in Your presence. Remind me that waiting with You is never wasted. Shape me in the stillness and prepare me for what You're doing next. In Jesus' name, amen.

Advent Application

Choose one area where you are waiting—large or small—and turn it into worship today. Each time it comes to mind, trade questions for trust with a simple prayer: "Lord, I believe Your timing is perfect." By day's end, note how this shift has shaped your heart.

December 5

LET YOUR LIGHT PIERCE THE DARKNESS

*The light shines in the darkness,
and the darkness can never extinguish it.*

JOHN 1:5

What stars are to the night sky, Christ's servants are to a darkened world. Light doesn't shout—it simply shines. It gives direction, attracts attention, and pierces through the darkness without a word. You don't have to announce it. Just be it. Whether you're on a team, at work, or in your neighborhood—you are the light in darkness. Don't hide it, don't limit it. Just let it shine.

— Charles R. Swindoll

Reflection

Today, the Advent flame burns brightly—no longer a flicker, but a steady and radiant glow. What began in the first devotional as a glimmer of hope—nurtured by trust, fed by Scripture, and anchored in God's perfect timing—has grown into a light that not only guides *you* but now shines *through* you.

Let me share a moment I won't forget. One morning, I rushed into the office, overwhelmed by deadlines and distracted by unspoken worries. As I settled at my desk, I noticed a sticky note on my computer screen. It was from one of my colleagues at IFL. In her handwriting were these words: *"Praying for you today. Your words are reaching places we may never see. Keep shining."*

It was simple—just ink on paper—but it lifted a heaviness I hadn't even realized I was carrying. Her gentle act of kindness reminded me that I wasn't invisible. I wasn't alone. Her unassuming yet sincere light pierced the dark cloud, and the warmth of that glow began to change my heart.

That's the thing about light. It simply shines. And that's exactly what Christ has called us to do. John's gospel boldly declares: *"The light shines in the darkness, and the darkness can never extinguish it"* (John 1:5). This is more than a poetic sentiment; it is granite truth. Jesus didn't come to decorate the darkness. He came to *defeat* it. His light broke into a world marked by sorrow and silence, and it hasn't stopped shining since.

And now, amazingly, that light shines *through us.* Not because we're powerful or perfect. Not because we always get it right. But because Jesus chooses to reflect His light through everyday people: cracked vessels, tired hearts, and quiet faithfulness. He's the light source. We're the reflectors.

You don't need a stage from which to shine. A kind word, a handwritten note, a whispered prayer, a quiet act of service—these are holy sparks that travel further than we know. If your hope feels strong today, let it overflow into someone else's life. Someone nearby may be praying for a flicker of light, and your presence might be God's answer.

If your own hope feels dim, take heart. Even the smallest flame breaks the darkness. You don't have to force the light; rather, choose faithfulness, and keep the light lifted. That's the beauty of hope: it begins quietly within us, yet it was never meant to stay hidden. Hope is both a gift and a calling, carried into a world still shadowed by fear, loss, and confusion.

So light your candle today—on mission as well as in remembrance. Let it remind you: *the light you reflect matters.* Your presence can push back the night for someone else. And in Christ, darkness never prevails. The Light has come. He will come again. And until then, by His Spirit, He lives in you.

Darkness doesn't need to fully envelop you to be real. The moment even the slightest spark of light appears, darkness flees, so reflect the light He shines through you. Do not hide it. Do not dim it. Shine.

As you place your hope in God's promises, peace can begin to take hold—not as the end of darkness but as the spark of His nearness within it. Carry this light into the night, and let peace be the quiet center that lights your path as you walk on.

Prayer

Lord, thank You for being the light in my darkness. Help me reflect Your light with faithfulness and humility. Let even the simplest actions reveal Your love and bring hope to others. In Jesus' name, amen.

Advent Application

Think of someone who may need a spark of light today and reach out: a message, a call, or a prayer. Then meditate on John 1:5. Let that truth steady your heart. The darkness can never extinguish the light of Christ. Now step into your day remembering this: His light shines through you.

PEACE

THE DAWN
OF **PEACE**

The Light That Gently Guides Our Steps

{ December 6–10 }

Hope lit the first candle. Now a steadier glow greets us: peace—the quiet strength of Christ's presence that guides our steps when the path is dim. When we lit the candle of hope, we remembered God's unwavering faithfulness even when the road ahead was unclear. Peace rarely comes by ending the storm; it appears in the storm as the nearness of Christ within us—a calm center that holds while the world keeps turning. The same Light that sparked hope now steadies our souls.

How do we hold on to peace when fear shouts louder than faith—when the storm rages not only outside but within?

I'll never forget the night our son Asher battled pneumonia. His fever would not break. Karla and I took turns—rotating between medicine, whispered prayers, and sleepless watches.

We were exhausted, and answers were scarce. Yet in those quiet hours, something sacred settled over us—not in sound but in presence. A peace deeper than silence wrapped around us. We were not alone.

> **He Himself is our peace, and in His presence, we are not merely comforted— we are transformed.**

Peace did not arrive because the fever vanished. In fact, the fever lingered. Peace came because God was near. He did not fix everything in an instant; He held us, *steadying our hearts*. This is the peace Christ gives. It isn't the hush of a summer afternoon; it is the stillness at the center of the storm.

Like a candle flickering in a gusty room, His peace may tremble, but it never goes out. It may not change the situation, but it changes us.

Scripture points us here. Zechariah, filled with the Holy Spirit, proclaimed:

"Because of God's tender mercy,
the morning light from heaven is about to break upon us,
to give light to those who sit in darkness and in the
shadow of death,
and to guide us to the path of peace." (Luke 1:78–79)

In the Bible, peace is more than the absence of trouble; it is the presence of wholeness. In Hebrew it is *shalom*. In Greek, it is *eirene*. Both speak of a deep, restorative calm that heals what is broken.

Centuries before Christ's birth, Isaiah prophesied the coming of a king—the Prince of Peace (Isaiah 9:6–7). That king is Jesus, the Everlasting Light. He offers more than a feeling or a concept; He Himself is our peace, and in His presence, we are not merely comforted—we are transformed.

As you journey through this second theme of Advent, light the candle of peace. At first, its glow may seem small, flickering in the cold and clamor of the season. Yet day by day, it grows, gently pushing back the shadows. That Light is Christ. He does more than brighten our path; He guides our feet into peace. Not temporary relief, but *shalom*—wholeness, healing, restoration. True peace doesn't wait for perfect conditions; it arrives with the presence of our perfect Savior. And wherever Christ is present, peace is not a distant hope—it is a living reality.

───────────────

Advent Wreath: Bethlehem Candle (Purple)

Symbolizes the peace of Christ and the journey of Mary and Joseph to Bethlehem

Nativity Action: Add Mary and Joseph to the scene.

Scripture Reading: Isaiah 40:3–5; Luke 1:78–79.

Reflection: As you light the second candle, ask: *Where do I need Christ's peace to settle the storm within me?* Let His presence calm your heart.

December 6

FINDING PEACE AMID YOUR STORM

When Jesus woke up, he rebuked the wind
and said to the waves, 'Silence! Be still!'
Suddenly the wind stopped,
and there was a great calm.

MARK 4:39

Peace isn't found in the absence of chaos—it's found in the presence of Christ. When we consciously lean on Him and abandon all our strength, He holds us up. Isaiah reminds us that God guards those with a steadfast frame of mind—those who trust, who lean, and who rest on Him alone (Isaiah 26:3). He doesn't always still the storm around us, but He speaks calm into the storm within us.

— Charles R. Swindoll

Reflection

The disciples were seasoned fishermen, well acquainted with the unpredictable waters of the Sea of Galilee. Storms were nothing new, and they knew how to navigate them. Yet this squall hit different—sudden, violent, and beyond their skill. Waves pounded their boat, wind tore through the sails, and water rose faster than their hands could bail. And Jesus? He was asleep—on a cushion, calm as dawn.

To the disciples, His quiet must have felt like abandonment. In their panic, they cried out, "Teacher, don't You care that we are going to drown?" Then Jesus rose, faced the gale, and spoke three simple words: *"Silence! Be still!"* Instantly, the wind died down, the waves smoothed, and a great calm settled—over the lake and over them.

This scene unveils a powerful truth: peace doesn't wait for the sky to clear; it steps into the storm when Jesus speaks. He didn't scan the horizon for better weather; He brought the calm with His word. His voice didn't react to the crisis; it ruled over it. This peace wasn't tied to outward conditions; it rests in His unshakable trust in the Father.

In Greek, Christ's command, *be still*, carries the sense of being muzzled—of a quiet that holds. The peace Jesus gives is not fragile or fleeting; it runs deep, steady, and durable because He is present.

Isaiah captured this promise:

> *You will keep in perfect peace*
> *all who trust in you,*
> *all whose thoughts are fixed on you!* (Isaiah 26:3)

We don't engineer that peace; we receive it as we rest in God's nearness. It steadies the mind and settles the soul.

We often plead with Jesus to change our situation. Often, He starts by changing us within it. True peace begins when we trust the One who's already in the boat.

Consider Daniel in the lions' den (Daniel 6). God did not remove him from danger; instead, His presence shut the mouths of the lions and surrounded Daniel with supernatural calm. Like the disciples, Daniel learned that true peace rises from God's nearness—even in the shadow of threat.

This biblical account reminds us that Jesus never panics, even when we do. He sees our fear, yet He is never cowed by it. The world says peace means trouble has left; Jesus shows that peace means *He has arrived.*

As Pastor Chuck wisely said, "Peace doesn't come from finding a lake with no storms. It comes from having Jesus in the boat."

So, what storm are you facing today? What waves threaten your sense of peace and stability? Advent whispers this truth: *Christ is with you.* You are not alone. You are not helpless. And no storm can overpower your Savior.

Let Him speak over your fear. Let His word do what only His word can do: *"Peace. Be still."* And when His voice breaks through the storm, you will find that the calm around you is nothing compared to the calm within you.

Prayer

Jesus, speak peace into the storm I face today. Let Your words still the chaos within me. Anchor my heart to Your promises; guard my mind with your perfect peace. Teach me to trust the certainty of Your presence rather than the stillness of my situation. Calm the storm inside me. Be my peace. Amen.

Advent Application

Find a quiet place and breathe deeply. Picture yourself in a storm-tossed boat with Jesus beside you, calm and unshaken. Let His presence quiet the chaos within and around you. Hear Him speak to your heart: *"Peace. Be still."* Name the storm you're facing and answer Him in a single sentence of trust. Write His words—and your response—in a journal; keep them with you today, and return to them whenever fear tries to rise again. Let His presence set your course, even when the weather shifts.

December 7

MAKE ROOM FOR PEACE

And while they were there [in Bethlehem],
the time came for her baby to be born.
She gave birth to her firstborn son.
She wrapped him snugly in strips of cloth
and laid him in a manger,
because there was no lodging available for them.

LUKE 2:6–7

Peace is the ability to remain faithful, even when your dreams are not fulfilled. If you forget that, you'll be frustrated, and your peace will quickly disappear. When I entrust my frame of mind to Him and lean on my everlasting Rock, He supports me with the ability to stay at the task as I let Him open the doors—in His time.

—Charles R. Swindoll

Reflection

We often imagine that peace will arrive when life finally slows down—when our calendars clear, our prayers are answered, or our long-awaited dreams at last come true. Yet Advent gently reminds us that peace is not the product of perfect conditions; it comes when we make room for Christ.

Last Christmas, my son Asher received a simple gift from a family who listens to our Spanish broadcast—a small plastic nativity set. To him, it was a treasure. He carefully set each little figure inside the stable, playing the music over and over again with wide-eyed wonder.

One afternoon, I noticed him struggling to place the baby Jesus in the crowded scene. The stable seemed full—no space left. Instead of removing anyone, Asher gently shifted the shepherds, nudged the animals, and nestled Jesus close to Mary and Joseph. Then he stepped back, satisfied: "Now there's room," he said. "I don't want Jesus to be left out."

That moment stopped me in my tracks. Without knowing it, Asher preached the heart of Christmas. *Peace doesn't simply appear; it grows in hearts willing to make space for it.* Peace comes when we rearrange our lives to welcome Christ.

Luke tells us, *"There was no room for them in the inn"* (Luke 2:7 NASB). That detail echoes through the centuries. The innkeeper wasn't hostile—only unavailable. Perhaps he was overwhelmed, perhaps busy beyond measure. In many ways, he represents us. We rarely reject Christ outright; we simply crowd Him out with everything else.

Mary and Joseph likely assumed they had time to travel, register, and return before the baby arrived. But the journey stretched longer than planned. By the time they reached Bethlehem, every room was taken. Only a crude shelter—likely a stable or cave—was offered. And there, in the stillness of a weary night, the Light of the World was born: wrapped in cloth, laid in a feeding trough, welcomed by a tired young couple clinging to God's promise. In that humble place, peace entered the world.

Centuries earlier, Isaiah had declared:

> *For to us a child is born,*
> *to us a son is given. . . .*
> *And he will be called . . .*
> *Prince of Peace.* (Isaiah 9:6 NIV)

That promise was fulfilled not in a palace but in a manger—among the willing rather than the powerful.

This is the holy paradox of Christmas: peace often comes where we least expect it—in the cluttered, ordinary stables of real life. And when we clear even a sliver of space for Jesus, His peace settles and stays.

Let's be clear: this Child was no ordinary child. As Mary cradled Him, she may have remembered the angel's words:

> *"You will conceive and give birth to a son, and you will name him Jesus. He will be very great and will be called the Son of the Most High. The Lord God will give him the throne of his ancestor David." (Luke 1:31–32)*

Could she have foreseen the cross? Likely not. Yet perhaps Simeon's prophecy still lingered in her heart: *"A sword will pierce your very soul"* (Luke 2:35). She may not have grasped the whole story, but she knew the Child—God's promised Lamb—and that was enough.

The manger was neither glamorous nor grand. It was simple, available, and offered shelter. And that changed everything. For where Christ is welcomed, peace doesn't just visit; it abides.

So how do we make room for Him? Begin by opening space in your schedule, your thoughts, and your affections. Loosen your grip on what clutters your heart. Peace isn't something we passively await; it's Someone we actively invite. And when we do, the same Light that filled a manger begins to shine within us.

Let us be like Asher's little stable—imperfect, yet open—willing to shift what needs shifting and ready to welcome Christ. Make room today, and let the Prince of Peace rule the space you surrender.

Prayer

Lord, my heart is crowded. Teach me to make space for You each day. Clear what competes for my attention. Let my heart become a manger where Your peace takes up residence. Amen.

Advent Application

Name one commitment you can release this week to make room for peace. Block into today's schedule fifteen unrushed minutes to sit quietly with Luke 2:6–7. Write a single sentence prayer: "Jesus, I make room for You here." Keep it with you, and return to it whenever hurry tries to take over. Let His presence set your pace.

December 8

QUIET YOUR HEART TO HEAR HIS VOICE

Be still, and know that I am God!

PSALM 46:10

Stillness is an essential part of growing deeper as we grow older. If we truly treasure quietness, we must make time for it—not just feed it our leftovers. God won't compete with our noise or pace. He waits to meet us in solitude, where agitation fades, petty problems shrink, and His presence becomes unmistakably real. In the quiet, God speaks, not to hurry us but to heal us. Peace and confidence come when we finally slow down and listen.

— Charles R. Swindoll

Reflection

Stillness is more than the absence of sound. It is the gentle hush of an early morning, the steady rhythm of breathing, and the sacred quiet where God's whisper can finally be heard. Amid the noise and rush of life, we discover peace as we intentionally quiet the heart to listen for His voice.

Psalm 46 does not depict tranquil skies and peaceful streams. Instead, it speaks of earthquakes, crumbling mountains, and nations in uproar. Yet, right in the center of that chaos, God declares: *"Be still, and know that I am God."*

This is not a passive suggestion. It is a divine invitation to cease striving and to remember the One who holds all things together. Stillness, then, is less about escape and more about surrender. It chooses trust even when everything around us shakes.

Several years ago, I entered a season marked by deep uncertainty. I sensed the Lord was leading me to step away from church planting— a ministry we deeply cherished but that had become unsustainable for both my family and my health. In response, we prayed, we waited, and we pursued opportunities. Yet for months, there was only silence. No clear direction emerged. I began to question: *Had I misunderstood God's leading? Was He speaking at all?*

Then came an unexpected invitation to interview at Dallas Theological Seminary. It was not the path I had envisioned, yet it felt like an open door placed before me. I accepted. While on campus, I confided in a friend about the silence and pressure I had been carrying. He listened, then spoke with quiet conviction: "Be still. Remember, God is in control." In that moment, those familiar words became a fresh confirmation of the Shepherd's voice—steady, guiding, and unmistakably leading me forward.

In the days that followed, I began to practice stillness, both outwardly and deep within. Each morning, I sat in silence, not to demand answers but to acknowledge God's presence. Gradually, the knots of fear loosened. I came to realize that God's silence had been preparing me. That stillness became sacred ground. It taught me to release my urge to fix everything and to wait with open hands and a trusting heart.

Shortly thereafter, an unplanned conversation opened a door I never expected: to return to serve full-time as lead pastor in the very ministry I had once left in obedience. This time, I returned with peace, clarity, and a deep awareness of God's perfect timing.

That season transformed me. I learned that God does not speak to rush us. *He speaks to restore us.* His direction often arrives in quiet places where trust takes root.

Psalm 46:10 reminds us that stillness is deliberate; we rest in the One who is sovereign. Stillness means shifting from control to surrender, from anxiety to assurance. It says, "God, even if I do not see the way forward, I trust that You do."

Let stillness lead you into surrender, and in that surrender, watch God make a way.

Prayer

Father, quiet my heart and steady my thoughts. Help me rest in Your presence and trust Your perfect timing. Teach me to be still—outwardly and within—so I can hear Your voice above the noise. In Jesus' name, amen.

Advent Application

Where can you carve out intentional space to hear God? Set aside ten quiet minutes today. Turn off your phone, sit comfortably, and close your eyes. Let your mind rest in His presence. Don't force anything— just listen. Write one sentence you sense Him impressing on your heart and carry it with you. Let this practice become your daily rhythm of surrender and stillness.

December 9

FIX YOUR MIND ON GOD'S FAITHFULNESS

You will keep in perfect peace
all who trust in you,
all whose thoughts are fixed on you!

ISAIAH 26:3

When we lean on God with a trusting mind-set, God will keep us in perfect peace. Isaiah used the word *shalom* twice. You, Lord, will watch over with *"shalom, shalom."* Not literally "perfect peace," but "peace, peace." In the Hebrew, a term is repeated for emphasis. So here the idea is of an unending security, a sense of uninterrupted, perpetual rest and calmness. It doesn't come from some human being . . . it comes from the God upon whom the person leans.

— Charles R. Swindoll

Reflection

When my son Asher was in second grade, he was nervous about a group presentation. As his teacher invited the class to write prayer requests, he scribbled, *"Lord, please help us in our group to talk about the project and not about other things."*

I smiled at his honesty. Yet that simple prayer stayed with me—it carried a quiet wisdom that keeps working on me. We all drift from what matters most. Just as Asher wanted his group to stay focused, God calls us to fix our minds on Him and keep them there.

So today, take a moment to ask yourself, *What is my mind fixed on? Are my thoughts anchored in trust or pulled toward fear, stress, and uncertainty?*

Peace does not spring from a flawless life; it grows as we center our hearts on the One who is flawless, unchanging, faithful, and near. When our thoughts are scattered, peace feels far away. But when we return our attention to God—again and again—He meets us with *shalom shalom*, a peace that quiets the soul and steadies the heart.

In Hebrew, *shalom* means more than just "peace." It speaks of wholeness, completeness, and deep well-being. When Isaiah repeats it—*shalom shalom*—he describes a peace that holds firm, even when life falls apart. It is not a fragile calm that evaporates with bad news or a hard day; it is a lasting strength that carries you through.

How do we find that peace? Isaiah tells us: *trust God completely*. Not as a one-time decision but as a daily posture. Fixing your mind on God doesn't mean pretending problems vanish; it means bringing your fears to Him and choosing His faithfulness as the place where your thoughts will rest. Under pressure, lean hard on the One who will not give way.

As we move through Advent—a season of hope and waiting—we lift our eyes to Jesus, the Everlasting Light. He stepped into a dark world to bring a light that cannot be overcome. While the world rushes and fills itself with noise, let the candle of peace burn steady within you:

> *The light shines in the darkness,*
> *and the darkness can never extinguish it.* (John 1:5)

Pastor Chuck says, "When you trust God, you refuse all other crutches." That kind of trust takes practice. It's a daily choice to lean your full weight on God with no backup plan. When you lean on Him, He may not give you quick answers—He will give you real peace that quiets your thoughts, holds you steady, and settles deep within you. It is more than peace; it is *shalom shalom*—flowing from Christ Himself, your light and your peace.

The promise is simple: *If you keep your mind fixed on Him, He will keep you in peace.* He does the keeping; we do the fixing. And the longer you look to Him, the brighter His Light becomes.

Prayer

Lord, steady my thoughts in You. When my mind wanders toward fear or control, draw me back to Your nearness. You are my Rock. You are my Light. I choose to trust You. Amen.

Advent Application

Let your thoughts return to Him—again and again. Whisper His name when you are driving. Offer a quiet prayer at your table and before you sleep. Linger in His Word. Let His Light flood your heart, and you'll discover a peace around you and within you.

December 10

EXPERIENCE PEACE BEYOND YOUR UNDERSTANDING

Don't worry about anything; instead, pray about everything.
Tell God what you need, and thank him for all he has done.
Then you will experience God's peace,
which exceeds anything we can understand.
His peace will guard your hearts and minds as you live in Christ Jesus.

PHILIPPIANS 4:6–7

Real peace comes only when you decide to take God at His word. When you trust God, you refuse all other crutches and lean your entire weight on the One who gives stable support. Can God hold you up? Yes! He's the Everlasting Rock. God will guard you with *shalom*—an unending security, uninterrupted rest, and complete calmness, surpassing all comprehension.

— Charles R. Swindoll

Reflection

Real peace begins when we trust God fully. It's not fleeting or fragile; it is a steady confidence rooted in the One who never fails. Can God hold you up? Absolutely. He is the Everlasting Rock. His peace—*shalom*—offers more than temporary relief. It brings a deep sense of safety, rest for the soul, and a calm that defies human explanation.

Years ago, the sponsors of an art competition asked painters to portray their idea of peace. Many submitted serene landscapes—sunsets, still lakes, golden fields. The winning canvas defied expectations: a violent storm: dark clouds swirling, lightning splitting the sky, trees bending in the wind, and waves crashing against a cliff. At first glance, it looked like chaos. But at the cliff's base, cradled in the crook of a windblown tree, rested a nest. Inside, a mother bird covered her chicks, calm, unshaken, at peace. Her stillness did not come from the absence of the storm; it came from the strength of the rock that held the tree and her nest secure.

That's the kind of peace Paul describes in Philippians 4:7—a peace that doesn't wait for the storm to pass and yet stands guard while the storm rages on. It's not weak or passive. It's active, like a soldier posted over your heart and mind. It doesn't just visit for a moment. It stays, shields, and steadies.

We often expect peace when life aligns—when health returns, when answers arrive, when certainty settles in. The peace of Christ, however, shows up in hospital rooms, in unanswered questions, and at midnight. Paul knew that peace from a prison cell. He wrote of a peace that *guards*. The Greek term for "guard" is *phroureo*, which implies military protection—like a city watched over through the night. That's what God's peace does: it keeps watch so fear does not overrun your heart and despair does not claim your mind.

Pastor Chuck says, "Real peace comes only when you decide to take God at His word." That requires faith—trusting when you don't have all the answers. Peace flows less from perfect understanding and more from nearness to Christ.

So place everything—your doubts, your fears, your future—into the hands of the One who already holds the outcome. That is *shalom*: a deep, anchored peace that remains even as winds rise.

Today, as Advent continues, we light the peace candle as more than tradition; it is a living testimony. Christ came to shine in the darkness. His light still glows in every heart that trusts Him.

Let His peace stand guard over your heart. Not because life is seamless, but because He is faithful. And as His peace settles in, listen. The next sound that rises is enduring *joy* born of His abiding presence. As you rest in Christ's peace, watch joy edge the horizon with light.

When peace takes root, joy becomes its first song—gladness that rises not from ease but from Immanuel's nearness. Tomorrow, light the candle of joy and let its music strengthen your steps.

Prayer

Jesus, I surrender what I can't control. Let Your peace guard my heart and mind. Even when I don't understand, help me trust in Your love and presence. Amen.

Advent Application

What anxiety or situation feels unresolved in your life right now? Write it down. Then turn that written worry into a short prayer of surrender: "Lord, I give this to You." Thank Him in advance for His faithfulness. Sit quietly for a few minutes and breathe this truth: "Your peace guards me." Then rise and take the next step—guarded by His peace and bright with His joy.

THE RADIANCE OF JOY

The Light That Kindles the Heart with Gladness

{December 11–15}

We have traced hope's first glimmer and felt peace steady our steps. Now, the light brightens into joy.

One afternoon, after a long day of back-to-back meetings and nonstop ministry, I came home feeling like a balloon that had lost all its air. All I wanted was stillness and silence. But my son Asher had other plans. With a spark in his eyes and the game *Sorry!* in his hands, he grinned and said, "I've been waiting for this all day, Papi!"

Ironically, *sorry* was exactly how I felt. I was tired, thin on patience, and in no shape for board games—yet we played. We laughed. And by the third round, the heaviness I carried slipped away. His joy didn't change my circumstances; it changed me.

That's the nature of joy—it doesn't require perfect conditions to appear. It simply needs a moment—a flicker—and a heart open enough to receive it.

Joy in Christ is like a candle in a dark room: one small flame pushes back the shadows and helps us see what we couldn't before. It can sound like laughter at a dinner table during hard times—delicate yet fiercely alive. Nurture that flame and it grows bright enough to outshine sorrow.

This joy isn't shallow or sentimental. It has depth because it's rooted in truth, anchored not in what is happening around us but in the One who walks beside us.

When the angel broke into the shepherds' night with heaven's declaration, it was a divine interruption: *"I bring you good news that will bring great joy to all people"* (Luke 2:10). The Joy-Bringer did not arrive with spectacle. He came wrapped in humility—Light cradled in a manger, radiating from the cry of a newborn King. Joy wasn't born in ease but from Presence: *Immanuel, God with us.*

Here lies the paradox of biblical joy—it blossoms amid sorrow, like dawn after a long night. It shows up in prison cells, in dry deserts, and in tear-soaked prayers. Joy is not denial; it is holy resilience—a sacred defiance against despair grounded in the nearness of Christ.

> **Here lies the paradox of biblical joy— it blossoms amid sorrow, like dawn after a long night.**

In the New Testament, the word for joy—*chara*—shares its root with *charis*, meaning grace. That's no coincidence. Joy springs from grace recognized. When we truly grasp that God chooses to dwell with us—even in our brokenness—joy does more than visit; it takes root.

The early church knew this well. Their joy was forged in hardship. Their gladness didn't rise and fall with outcomes; it was anchored in the resurrection. Jesus never promised an easy life, but He did promise His presence—and His presence gives birth to joy.

So this week, light the candle of joy. Not because life is tidy or easy but because Christ has come and remains with us. And where Christ is, joy is a strong living flame, always within reach, kindling hearts until the room is bright.

——◄◆►·-•-·◄◆►————◄◆►·-•-·◄◆►————◄◆►·-•-·◄◆►——

Advent Wreath: Shepherds Candle (Rose)

Symbolizes the joy announced to the shepherds and the growing excitement of Christ's arrival

Nativity Action: Add the shepherds and sheep.

Scripture Reading: Luke 2:8–14.

Reflection: As you light the third candle of joy, ask: *What unexpected place is God using to spark joy in me this week?* Let gratitude awaken joy again.

December 11

FIND JOY IN THE UNEXPECTED

*Mary responded,
"Oh, how my soul praises the L*ORD*.
How my spirit rejoices in God my Savior!"*

LUKE 1:46–47

Joy is an attitude determined by confidence in God, who is at work and in control, allowing all things to happen for one ultimate purpose: His greater glory. When Christ becomes our central focus— our reason for existence—contentment replaces anxiety, fears, and insecurities. Most people think happiness happens to them rather than something they diligently pursue. Joy comes to those who determine to pursue it despite everyday circumstances.

— Charles R. Swindoll

Reflection

I remember one especially stressful day in the recording studio. We were behind schedule, the script was still changing, and tension filled the air. As I stepped into the booth, adjusting my headphones, I noticed a handwritten note taped to the microphone: *"God is using your voice to reach someone today."* That small, unexpected gesture cut through my exhaustion like first light after a storm. In that moment, joy found a way in because someone chose to speak life into the chaos.

Joy often appears just like that: quiet, surprising, and unannounced. Mary certainly didn't anticipate her life being upended overnight. She wasn't looking for divine interruption; she was likely going about her daily chores, holding dreams of a future with Joseph. Then the angel Gabriel appeared with unimaginable news: she would carry the Messiah.

Mary's question was honest: *"But how can this happen? I am a virgin"* (Luke 1:34). Her situation invited misunderstanding, suspicion, and likely disgrace. And yet, her response was immediate and faith-filled: *"May it be done to me according to your word"* (Luke 1:38 NASB). The phrase *may it be done* is from the Greek word *ginomai*, which conveys the sense of surrender—*let it become so.* Mary didn't understand it all, but she trusted the One who did.

Her praise, recorded in Luke 1:46–55—known as the *Magnificat*—was not sung from comfort but from courage. A teenaged girl, uncertain of the future, chose to rejoice because she trusted God's character more than her circumstances. Her joy did not lean on clarity; it rose from confidence in God.

Advent joy is like that. It does not wait for every answer; it blooms while questions remain. It sings even in the dark. We often imagine joy as the reward after the resolution—after the diagnosis clears, the relationship heals, or the plan unfolds. Yet Scripture invites us to a deeper joy that begins with revelation before resolution. Joy is birthed when we recognize *God's presence in the unexpected.*

Mary teaches us that God's interruptions are often divine invitations. She bore the weight of whispered accusations, the risk of rejection, and the mystery of divine responsibility. Yet through it all, she embraced her calling with a willing heart. The miracle was not only that she carried Christ, but that she said yes—and kept saying yes.

Her response echoed the faithful of Israel, who had waited generations for their Messiah. And now, in the fullness of time, God kept His promise—not with fanfare but through the quiet obedience of a girl from Nazareth. Her joy was prophetic, a declaration that God had not forgotten His people.

What if the unexpected places in your life—those interruptions, detours, or delays—are the very places where God wants to birth something new? What if, like Mary, you are being invited to choose joy by trusting the One who calls you, even before you see how the path will unfold?

Christ, our Everlasting Light, does not wait for order to arrive; He steps into our chaos with purpose. Where Christ is present, joy breaks through and keeps shining.

Prayer

Lord, in moments that catch me off guard, help me lean into You. When my plans fall apart, remind me that You are still the author of my story. Let joy rise—not from what I understand but from who You are. Amen.

Advent Application

What unexpected place in your life might God use to birth new joy today? Invite Him into that space. Like Mary, respond with a willing yes and a rejoicing heart—and let the light of Christ shine there.

December 12

DRAW STRENGTH FROM JOY

*Don't be dejected and sad,
for the joy of the LORD is your strength!*

NEHEMIAH 8:10

Joy springs by viewing the day's events from eternity's perspective. With this intentional focus, you're sure to see today differently—with more joy and conviction that God is at work in your life. Remember, God remains in charge of your days and will faithfully develop His character in you. His joy will be your strength.

— Charles R. Swindoll

Reflection

Joy is strength—deep, quiet, steady, and unyielding in the face of difficulty.

Years ago, while serving in a small Guatemalan village, I met Leticia. Her home was simple, without electricity or running water, yet her spirit radiated a warmth that drew people in. I asked how she remained so hopeful. Smiling, she pointed to her worn Bible and said, "Because Jesus is here. And He never leaves." That one line has stayed with me ever since. Leticia's joy didn't depend on comfort; *it was rooted in Christ's presence.*

That encounter reminded me that joy can thrive in the most unlikely soil. Joy grows from the unshakable truth that even when life quakes beneath us, our foundation in Christ remains firm. Joy is the steady awareness that Jesus is near.

Advent is a season of holy tension. Darkness lingers. Answers are slow to come. And hope can feel fragile, like a single candle flickering in the wind. Yet right here, in the waiting, God offers something both powerful and surprising: *joy.* He gives joy not to distract us from pain but to strengthen us in it.

It's tempting to believe we must manufacture joy—to push through pain with a smile or sing through tears out of obligation. But Scripture points us to a different reality: *"The joy of the LORD is [our] strength"* (Nehemiah 8:10). It is His joy, not ours, that sustains.

Let this truth settle deep into your soul: the joy that holds you up isn't something you must produce; *it flows from the heart of God.* A God who, as Zephaniah promises, "will rejoice over you with joyful songs" (Zephaniah 3:17).

We often think joy is something we bring to God, as though we need to arrive cheerful before entering His presence. But Advent reminds us that true joy is something God brings to us—His delight, His steadfast gladness—even when life feels unfinished. When Nehemiah spoke those words—*"the joy of the LORD is your strength"*—he wasn't addressing people at a festival. He spoke to a weary, broken community standing among the ruins of Jerusalem. Their world was in pieces, yet they were called to rejoice. Why? Because joy would not be the prize after rebuilding, it would be the power to rebuild.

This is the quiet power of Advent: *Christ came not with spectacle but with presence.* His Light—gentle, persistent, and eternal—still shines, piercing the dark instead of waiting for it to lift.

So if you're tired today, do not manufacture a smile. Receive His joy, strength, and unshakable presence. Let it rise in you like a river fed by a spring that never runs dry. Even when you feel empty, you are not alone, and where Christ is, joy keeps flowing.

Prayer

Lord, thank You that my strength rests not on how I feel but on the joy You give. When I'm weary, remind me that You sing over me. Let Your joy be the foundation of my life—steady, deep, and overflowing. Fill every empty space with Your presence and Your peace. Amen.

Advent Application

Where are you leaning on your own strength today? Pause and name that place. Invite God into it—ask Him to fill it with His joy. Then reflect on three occasions His joy has carried you through difficulty. Write them down. Thank Him for His faithfulness and choose to trust Him again today. Rise in His strength—let the joy of the Lord do the lifting.

December 13

RECOGNIZE JOY IN YOUR WAITING

Soon afterward his wife, Elizabeth, became pregnant
and went into seclusion for five months.
"How kind the LORD is!" she exclaimed.
"He has taken away my disgrace of having no children."

LUKE 1:24–25

J oy doesn't refer to superficial happiness or shallow cheerfulness. Joy is a deeply felt contentment that transcends difficult circumstances and derives maximum enjoyment from every good experience. Deep, contented joy comes from a place of complete security and confidence—even in the midst of trials. As I once heard, "Joy is the flag that flies over the castle of our hearts, announcing that the King is in residence."

— Charles R. Swindoll

Reflection

Years ago, as Pastor Chuck and I stood near the Christmas tree inside the IFL building, he smiled and quietly said, "Sometimes, Carlos, joy looks like remembering why we started." That simple truth still lingers. Life and ministry can grow complicated, yet joy often reappears when we pause and remember the foundation beneath all: *Christ came.* And that alone is enough.

Waiting is rarely something we choose. More often, it chooses us. Whether you're waiting for healing, restoration, clarity, or long-anticipated answers, the waiting room of life can feel both heavy and hollow.

Elizabeth knew that ache intimately. In her culture, childlessness was personal grief and public shame. In a world that measured worth by visible blessing, for years she carried the stigma of being barren. Yet Scripture tells us that she and her husband Zechariah were *"righteous in God's eyes"* (Luke 1:6). Though God seemed silent, Elizabeth remained faithful—praying, hoping, and believing.

Then, in the quiet of the temple, Zechariah encountered the angel Gabriel. The message was breathtaking: Elizabeth, now advanced in years, would bear a son—and not just any son. John the Baptist would prepare the way for the Messiah. In one moment, God broke Elizabeth's silence and Israel's. After four centuries without prophetic voice, heaven's words returned, announcing good news once again.

Elizabeth responded with reverence. She withdrew in quiet worship, letting joy take root in the hidden place. Her words, though few, brim with gratitude: *"How kind the Lord is!"* (Luke 1:25) No fanfare. Just humble awe. Her example whispers across the centuries: some joys are too sacred to broadcast; they are meant to be treasured in stillness until the right time to speak.

Advent meets us in that same stillness. It reminds us that God is not absent in the silence; often, He's most active beneath the surface. Joy doesn't always arrive with trumpets; it can slip in like a whisper, like sunrise breaking over cold hills. And even when answers delay, joy can still be found in the One who holds us.

Scripture reveals that joy is a companion in the waiting room of faith. Elizabeth waited decades. Israel waited generations. And when the time was right, God remembered His promise. He always does. God's delays are not denials. Often the miracle is more than provision; it is the transformation He works in us while we wait.

Christ, our Everlasting Light, is present in the shadows, and in His presence true joy shines.

So pause today in reverence. What if, like Elizabeth, you whispered, *"How kind the Lord is,"* not because everything is resolved but because God is here, still working, still kind.

Prayer

Lord, help me recognize Your kindness in the places that still feel unfinished. When I grow weary in waiting, remind me that Your timing is perfect, and Your presence is constant. Teach my heart to rejoice before I see the outcome, trusting that Your nearness is enough. Amen.

Advent Application

Where are you waiting today? What area of your life feels unresolved? Rather than rushing toward resolution, create space for reverence. Light a candle. Take a quiet walk. Reflect on this question: *Where has God already been present in this season?* Name it. Then raise that memory like a banner and keep waiting with joy.

December 14

LET YOUR JOY OVERFLOW

*I pray that God, the source of hope,
will fill you completely with joy and peace
because you trust in him.*

ROMANS 15:13

Joy is a matter of attitude that stems from one's confidence in God—that He is at work, that He is in full control, that He is in the midst of whatever has happened, is happening, and will happen. Either we fix our minds on that and determine to laugh again, or we wail and whine our way through life, complaining that we never got a fair shake.

— Charles R. Swindoll

Reflection

One unforgettable afternoon, I visited a young couple new to our church. Their home was modest, their furniture well-worn, but their hospitality radiated warmth. She served sweet bread and coffee while he shared how Jesus had transformed their lives. Their laughter filled the room like music. In that unassuming space, I witnessed something profound: *joy*. Not flashy or perfect, but humble, generous, and grace-rooted.

That kind of joy doesn't come from comfort; rather, it flows from trust. You see it most in people whose paths are rough—people anchored in the unshakable goodness of God.

Joy isn't a personality trait or a passing emotion. It's a spiritual reality: a posture of the heart that believes God is near and actively working, even in the mess. That's the kind of joy Paul envisions when he prays that *"God, the source of hope, will fill you completely with joy and peace because you trust in him"* (Romans 15:13). This is no spark; it is a steady filling that spills into our words, our service, and our love.

Here's the truth: *we can't overflow if we're running on empty*. And many of us are drained by deadlines, weighed down by grief, dulled by disappointment, overwhelmed by noise. We scroll, strive, and survive . . . yet seldom pause to be filled.

Advent meets us in that exhaustion. It invites us to slow down, breathe deeply, and open ourselves to receive what only God can give: hope, peace, and joy in full measure.

Paul reminds us that God is not just the object of our hope—He is its source. It is about resting in the truth that God is near, faithful, and fully present—even in the hard places where everything isn't fine.

Advent draws our attention back to Jesus—our Everlasting Light. He is not a seasonal ornament, but a Savior who stepped into real darkness. His light doesn't dim when our circumstances change. He fills the empty spaces with Himself, offering joy, peace, and purpose.

Jesus is the Savior we trust for eternity, and He's the Light we lean on each day. In weakness, He is our strength. In waiting, He is our peace. In weariness, He is the joy that steadies our soul.

And this joy is not meant to be stored away—it's meant to spill over. Every kind word, every quiet prayer, every small act of compassion becomes a beam of light in someone else's darkness. That's the quiet call of Advent: *Be filled. Then shine.*

You don't need a perfect life to overflow with joy. Open your hands to be filled, and open your life to let that joy become someone else's strength.

Prayer

I confess I often try to make my own joy. Fill me again with Your joy, Your peace, and Your presence. Let what You pour in overflow through me, not only to bless me but to bring light to others today. Amen.

Advent Application

Pause today and ask yourself: *Am I living filled, or am I just functioning?* Let God refill you through prayer, Scripture, or quiet time in His presence. Then, think of someone who may be weary, and choose one simple act of joy—send a kind message, offer to pray, or deliver a small gift. Move joy from your heart to your hands, and let it spill into someone else's day.

December 15

SHARE THE NEWS OF GREAT JOY

But the angel reassured them.
"Don't be afraid!" he said.
"I bring you good news that will bring great joy to all people.
The Savior—yes, the Messiah, the LORD—
has been born today in Bethlehem, the city of David!"

LUKE 2:10-11

Don't be afraid! . . . I bring you good news that will bring great joy to all people." These familiar ancient words echoed in the night sky as it was brightened by the appearance of God's angels. But this announcement came not to a king or a commander or anyone of renown but to lowly, dirty shepherds. The angels were serious when they said this good news was for *all* people.

— Charles R. Swindoll

Reflection

The announcement came suddenly. An ordinary night burst open with extraordinary light. A group of weary, overlooked shepherds—men considered socially and spiritually insignificant—were the first to hear the greatest proclamation in human history: *"I bring you good news that will bring great joy to all people"* (Luke 2:10). This was no shallow happiness, no fleeting seasonal cheer. This was great joy—deep, abiding, and universal. God entrusted the message to the humble and unseen, not to courts or councils.

The angel's opening words were striking: *"Don't be afraid!"* (2:10)—as if to say, *"This joy is for you!"* You are seen. You are safe. You are invited. This is the heart of Advent—Christ came for the frightened, the grieving, the searching, and the unseen.

The joy of that night had a name: *Jesus*. He wasn't born in luxury; He arrived in humility and was laid in a manger. The Prince of Peace came without spectacle, yet with quiet glory—a Light that still pierces the dark.

Don't miss what the shepherds did next: *they moved*. They didn't stay frozen in awe. They went. They found. They told. Joy compelled them to act, and it still does. Their joy became a testimony because they refused to keep silent.

Why shepherds? Why not rulers or rabbis? Because God was making a statement: *This Savior is for all people, even the forgotten.*

According to longstanding tradition, the shepherds who guarded lambs for temple sacrifice were the first to behold the *"Lamb of God who takes away the sin of the world"* (John 1:29, emphasis added). The field outside Bethlehem—now known as Shepherds' Field—was the very place where heaven's glory split the sky and proclaimed the birth of the Final Sacrifice—Jesus, who came to give His life for us.

Centuries of waiting culminated not in a palace, but in a stable. We might have chosen a five-star suite; God gave a single star and a manger overflowing with mercy. And still today, the message remains the same: *"Good news! Great joy! For all people!"*

In a season full of songs and traditions, we may sing about joy yet forget to share it. Advent calls us deeper—to receive joy and then reflect it. Sometimes that means speaking a kind word, offering forgiveness or simply showing up for someone who feels forgotten. Joy is not the absence of sorrow—it's the presence of the Savior.

As we close this Advent week centered on joy, remember this truth: joy dims when hoarded and shines when shared. Shared joy makes room for the greatest gift: *love*.

True joy in Christ moves us from self-focus toward compassion, action, and grace-filled presence in a noisy, hurting world. Joy that abides will not sit still; it turns outward as love—love that draws near, bears burdens, and shines in the ordinary. Let the next candle warm your heart toward others.

So, let Christ's joy steady your steps and brighten your path. Let His light be the compass of your days. And as joy begins to sing in your soul, watch how it blossoms into love—rising like dawn, warm and generous, too radiant to keep to yourself. Love becomes the next word on your tongue, the next gift in your hand, the next act of grace in your day. For joy finds its fullness only when it overflows into love.

Prayer

Jesus, thank You for the joy You brought into our world—joy wide enough to reach every story. Help me carry that joy with open hands and an open heart. Use me today to reflect Your light into someone else's darkness. Amen.

Advent Application

Ask God to place someone on your heart today—someone who needs a touch of Christ's joy. Write his or her name and one specific act you will take. Take an intentional step to reflect God's light—through a note, a call, a kind gesture, or your quiet presence. Don't store the good news—deliver it before the day is done.

LOVE

THE FLAME
OF LOVE

⌒∾⌒

The Light That Warms the Soul with Eternal Reach

{ December 16–20 }

We have watched hope ignite, felt peace steady our steps, and seen joy brighten the room. Now the light draws us deeper to love, the very heart of Advent. This is the flame of love, the Light that warms the soul with eternal reach. Love is more than a passing feeling; it is a divine light—Christ, our Everlasting Light—bridging the vast distance between heaven's perfection and earth's brokenness.

This love is not passive. It acts, sacrifices, and radiates. The same Light that offered us hope, peace, and joy now beckons us into the Father's embrace: a love that stoops low, gives generously, and restores fully. Yet in weary moments, when we feel unworthy or unseen, a quiet question arises: *Can such love truly reach me?*

I remember a few years ago, Karla and I walked through a draining season—tight schedules, unexpected challenges, and soul-deep exhaustion. One morning, already late and frayed, I noticed she had packed our son's lunch, set out coffee, and sent a brief devotional ending with, *"I'm praying for you. I love you."* That morning, love did not surge as emotion; it arrived as a choice. A small, faithful act reflected God's heart: a love that meets us where we are, especially when we have nothing left to give.

God's love is like a porch light left on for a child returning home. It doesn't force its way in; it waits—steady and unwavering—casting a gentle glow that whispers, *"You're not alone. You're welcome here."* True love shows up where we are without demanding attention. Like soft light spilling into the dark night, God's love pierces through shame and fear, offering presence instead of punishment.

> **In Christ, love wrapped itself in flesh, stepped into our mess, and chose redemption over condemnation.**

The fourth candle reminds us that divine love moves first when the time is right. It doesn't require us to be ready or flawless. In Christ, love wrapped itself in flesh, stepped into our mess, and chose redemption over condemnation. This is love made visible—love incarnate.

Too often, we treat love as a prize earned by worth or effort. God's love breaks that pattern. It is constant, proactive, and completely unmerited.

As Advent progresses and the wreath grows brighter, the fourth candle invites us to dwell on love: a steady flame that crosses every boundary and points us toward the One at the very center.

Soon we will light the Christ candle, symbolizing the truest source of that love—the Light in whom all hope, peace, joy, and love find their fullness. The apostle John wrote,

> *God showed us how much he loved us by sending his one and only Son into the world so that we might have eternal life through him.* (1 John 4:9)

This is *agape* love—a love that enters in, gives everything, and asks for nothing in return. It doesn't merely comfort; it transforms.

So as you light the fourth candle, pause. Let its glow speak to your soul. Love has a name—*Immanuel.* Love came first. And now Love calls you to carry His flame into a world still waiting for His warmth.

As this love burns steady within you, lift your eyes. Watch for the arrival—brilliant as sunrise, unstoppable as morning—until every shadow disappears. The Everlasting Light has stepped into the world, not in story or symbol but in flesh and blood, dwelling with us. Love is more than an Advent theme; it is the heartbeat of the gospel—received, reflected, carried. Enter Christmas as both the found and the sent. Welcome His love, shine His light, and let the arrival blaze through you.

***

Advent Wreath: Angels Candle (Purple)

Symbolizes the love of God proclaimed by the angels and fulfilled in Christ's birth

Nativity Action: Place the barn animals and prepare the manger.

Scripture Reading: Luke 1:26–38.

Reflection: As you light the fourth candle, ask: *How is God inviting me to embody His love this week?* Let your love reflect His light.

December 16

MARVEL AT LOVE MADE FLESH

*So the Word became human
and made his home among us.
He was full of unfailing love and faithfulness.*

JOHN 1:14

Two millennia ago, God answered humanity's anguished cry by making "the problem of evil" His own. Almighty God became Immanuel—"God with us." He lived as we live, suffered as we suffer, died as we die, yet without sin. Jesus, who left heaven, took on human flesh, lived on earth a little over thirty-three years, and modeled the life of God. What characterized Him? Two things: self-sacrifice and a fragrant aroma of love.

— Charles R. Swindoll

Reflection

Years ago, as I was preparing to record a message for our radio broadcast, I remember Pastor Chuck stepped quietly into the studio and said, "Carlos, let your tone carry your heart as much as your content." That phrase was more than advice; it was a reminder that love isn't always loud. Often, its clearest note is heard in the way we speak. In both ministry and life, truth without love turns to noise. Love spoken clearly, calmly, and with kindness has the power to move mountains and melt hearts.

In Jesus Christ, the eternal Word became flesh and moved into the neighborhood. He walked our streets, sat at our tables, and stood beside our graves. He came all the way in. He dwelt among us, suffered for us, and died to redeem us—embodying a love so radiant it could only be divine. His life bore two hallmarks: *self-giving* and *steadfast love*, enduring and fragrant like costly perfume poured out without reserve.

We often picture love as soft and serene: candlelit moments, handwritten notes, warm embraces. Yet the love that arrived at Advent was far more daring. It wasn't passive or poetic; it was powerful, purposeful, and costly. The love of Christ is not a fleeting emotion but a fierce, radiant force. It doesn't linger at a safe distance but draws close and takes on flesh.

The Everlasting Light broke through our darkness with unwavering brilliance, clothed in humility rather than pomp.

John wrote, *"The Word became human and made his home among us"* (John 1:14). That's incarnation. God didn't send a message; He sent Himself. The One who spoke galaxies into being cried in a manger.

The Infinite became an infant. This isn't soft theology; it's sacred mystery. And it demands more than admiration. It calls for awe.

Why would God step into our mess? Because love moves toward the wounded. Jesus left the safe heights of heaven and stepped down, took on flesh, and made our burden His own. He chose vulnerability for the vulnerable.

He came as one of us—entering our hunger, our weakness, our hidden places. This is love with skin on. His humility took shape in history: a manger, a village, a cross. It left marks—calloused hands, tear-wet cheeks, nail-pierced wrists. Love came close enough to be scarred and close enough to save.

So how do we love like that? We begin small. Sit with someone who feels invisible. Choose silence instead of a sharp retort. Offer forgiveness when pride demands a grudge. To marvel at His love is to mirror it—in kitchens, conversations, and quiet acts of care. Incarnation isn't just doctrine; it is a daily invitation to bend low, listen deep, and love well.

That same Spirit of Incarnate Love still lives among us. We find it not only in pews or polished prayers but in hospital rooms, unexpected kindnesses, hard-won forgiveness, and quiet faithfulness.

Gospel love kneels. It weeps. It waits. It stays. It stands close. It's not driven by ease but compelled by presence.

Advent, then, is not about cozy nostalgia or seasonal warmth. It's about remembering the fierce faithfulness of our God who chose to become breakable. It's about marveling—not just at the baby in the manger but at the unimaginable humility of God. The God who came close, became interruptible, reachable, touchable. Jesus didn't shout salvation from the skies. He whispered it through every act of compassion, every drop of blood.

This is the miracle of Christmas: *God came*, and *He stayed*. Love didn't pass through; it took up residence. And in doing so, God redefined love for us.

This Advent, love might not look like warm lights or wrapped gifts. It might look like sitting silently beside someone in grief. It might mean forgiving when resentment feels justified. It might require real, sacrificial presence in places you'd rather avoid. Because that's what Jesus did. He came close. He stayed. And the Spirit of God remains.

God is not far off. He is here. In Christ, love moved into the neighborhood and never left. Open your door—let His love take up residence in you, and let your life prove He is here.

Prayer

Jesus, Word made flesh, thank You for coming near—for stepping into my world, not as an idea but as a living presence. Let Your love make its home in me and teach me to shine with Your light where I live today. Amen.

Advent Application

Light a candle today—not for decoration but as a declaration: *The Light has come, and it remains.* Let that truth warm your heart and guide your hands and steps.

December 17

FOLLOW THE LIGHT INTO HUMILITY

Though he was God, he did not think of equality with God as something to cling to. Instead, he gave up his divine privileges; he took the humble position of a slave and was born as a human being.

PHILIPPIANS 2:6–7

Existing in unchanging deity of His essence, Jesus did not regard that position in heaven something He would hold on to and not release. Why? Because He is humble of heart. Because to come to our rescue, He couldn't remain in heaven. He let go of His privileged position where He received angelic praise, knew no pain, experienced no rejection. Unclutching His divine nature, Jesus became a servant.

— **Charles R. Swindoll**

Reflection

One quiet Sunday after service, María—a woman from our church—pressed a small bag of homemade tamales into my hands. "You remind me I'm not forgotten," she whispered. Only then did I see the thread: week after week I had asked about her life, remembered her story, prayed with her. She had also noticed something about me—that I love homemade tamales—and this was her way of saying, "I see you too." In that simple exchange, love took a humble, tangible shape.

That moment taught me that love seldom thunders; it keeps showing up. It learns a name, remembers a preference, brings a meal. Heaven's story moves this way: *The Light chose the low road*. To follow Christ is to follow His Light along the same humble path—through small, steady acts that say, "You are seen," and in saying it, make Him seen.

We often think love must be loud, measured by grand gestures or dramatic rescues. Yet heaven's love arrives in whispers, wrapped in the ordinary—a visit, a listening ear, a simple plate of tamales prepared by hands the world overlooks. Such love avoids the spotlight yet reshapes hearts. This is the heart of Advent: *God with us*, drawing near in ways we can touch and taste, and in ways we might miss unless we look.

And that is precisely why the humility of Jesus startles us. The ordinary is not a detour but the King's chosen road. What kind of King leaves His throne to share our table? What kind of God trades angelic praise for human misunderstanding and rejection? In a world chasing platforms and performance, Jesus chooses manger before throne, towel before title, cross before crown. To follow His light is to walk that same humble way.

In his letter to the Philippians, Paul writes a stunning truth about Christ Jesus:

> *Though he was God,*
>   *he did not think of equality with God*
>   *as something to cling to.* (Philippians 2:6)

God released His divine privileges. He emptied Himself—not of deity but of entitlement and not of power but of the rights He could have rightly held.

This humility doesn't simply inspire admiration; it calls for transformation. True humility, modeled by Jesus, is power held with restraint. It is strength surrendered for the sake of love. It is love that stoops. It is Light bending low into our dust. And in that dust—our dust—He revealed a glory the world had never imagined: God serving, riding a donkey, washing feet, and hanging on a cross.

To follow the Light into humility is to choose self-giving love over self-preservation. It means living open-handed in a world that clutches tightly. It means valuing quiet obedience over public validation. Paul calls us, *"You must have the same attitude that Christ Jesus had"* (2:5). This is not abstract theology—it's an invitation to embody Christlike love.

This is the paradox of the kingdom: *the way up begins by going low. The path to greatness runs through acts of service.*

Jesus didn't lead from above, He led from alongside. He didn't avoid our pain, He entered it. When we follow Him there, we don't lose ourselves; we discover who we were made to be.

This Advent, as we draw near the manger, we approach more than a baby wrapped in cloth—we encounter God wrapped in humility. The Eternal stepped into time. The Creator entered creation.

The Light kindled in our darkness so we would never walk it alone. If Jesus—the Light of the World, the King of heaven—chose humility to draw near to us, how much more should humility draw us near to others?

María's tamales were more than a meal; they were a warm parable of Advent—love arriving quietly, close enough to taste. In her simple gift, humility took on a shape I could hold, reminding me that Christ's light often travels the low road of ordinary kindness.

Advent isn't only about remembering that Christ came; it's about reflecting *how* He came—in a posture of surrender, gentleness, and nearness. Let His posture become your pattern.

This season, admire the humility of Jesus *and* practice it until His presence is unmistakable in the way you love. Bring the meal. Make the call. Carry the towel. Let someone taste grace and know he or she is not forgotten.

Prayer

Jesus, humble King, You gave up everything to draw near to us. Teach me that the path to true life is the path You walked—marked by surrender, service, and love. Help me not just speak of humility, but live it. Let Your Light shine through me as I lay down my pride and lift others up. Amen.

Advent Application

Where is God inviting you to "descend" this season—to yield, to listen, to serve? Is there a relationship or situation where Christ's humility could reshape your response? Choose one concrete act of quiet service today. Bend low, show up, and let humility carry His light into that place.

December 18

RECEIVE THE GIFT OF GOD'S LOVE

God showed how much he loved us
by sending his one and only Son into the world
so that we might have eternal life through him.
This is real love—not that we loved God,
but that he loved us and sent his Son as a sacrifice
to take away our sins.

1 JOHN 4:9–10

Every Christmas, God announces to every one of us the three words that are most important to hear. He says to us, "I love you." Through lights that glow, songs that proclaim, and gifts that reflect generosity, He reminds us: "My Son came and died for you." It's more than a season. It's a sacred invitation to receive a love worth waiting for—freely given, undeserved, and eternal.

—Charles R. Swindoll

Reflection

Some of the hardest people to love are those who quietly believe they don't deserve it, and sometimes one of those people is the one in the mirror.

Years ago, during a particularly painful season in my early days as a Spanish pastor, I made a decision that deeply wounded someone I loved and respected. The weight of that failure felt crushing. Shame followed me like a shadow. I was certain I had disappointed God beyond repair, and I was ready to walk away from ministry altogether.

I sat in Pastor Chuck's office, barely able to explain why I no longer felt worthy to serve. He listened with that steady compassion of his. Then he leaned in and said words I'll never forget: *"Carlos, God's love doesn't expire when you fall. That's when it shows up stronger."*

He wasn't excusing my failure; he was magnifying grace—grace that moves toward us at our lowest. I didn't need to earn my way back into God's favor. I needed to receive the love that had never let go. That is where Advent meets us best: *not in our polished victories but in our unguarded places*. Christmas declares that God moved first—and His love still moves.

So don't resist it today. Don't hide the parts of yourself you think are too messy or too broken. Bring your whole self into His light and let Him love you there. When you truly know you are loved by God, it changes how you live, how you forgive, and how you love.

Throughout this Advent journey, we've lit candles for hope, peace, and joy. Now we arrive at love—not a sentiment but the fierce, self-giving love that reshaped eternity. The love born in Bethlehem, nailed to a cross, and raised in glory.

Christmas isn't just about remembering love; it's about encountering it. The Light of the World didn't slip into history as a pleasant idea. Jesus wasn't merely born. He was sent on a mission. The manger wasn't a quaint symbol; it was the first step in the greatest rescue mission the world has ever known— *the redemption of humanity.*

God doesn't love us because we are lovable. He loves us because He is love. His love doesn't awaken in response to our beauty, and it doesn't fade in response to our brokenness. It doesn't withdraw from our weakness; it draws near. Jesus came wrapped not in royal robes but in humility. Why? Because real love stoops. Real love serves. Real love sacrifices.

In a world that distorts love into convenience or performance, Christ came to restore its meaning. Love is not passive. It moves toward. It mends. It remains.

And here's the most stunning truth: God's love didn't end at Christmas. It's alive today!

The incarnation proclaims it.

The cross confirms it.

The resurrection secures it.

Receive it—and let it remake you.

Let His love reach the parts of you still aching for healing. Then pass it on, because love received must become love extended. If we are truly formed by Christ's love, we will spend our lives giving it away—lifting others up, serving without applause, and leading hearts back to the Light that never dims.

Let this season's lights illuminate your heart, not just decorate your home. In Christ, the Everlasting Light has come. In His love, you are already home.

God's love is not something we earn or perform our way into; it is something we open our hearts to. Advent does not tell us to climb to heaven to reach God. It tells us He came down to reach us—into our need, our mess, our humanity. And now, His love waits right where we are. If you've ever wondered whether God still wants you—He does.

Christmas forever answers the question, "Does God love me?" He came. He stayed. And He still says, "I love you"—not because you have done everything right but because He is everything good. Open your heart, receive His love, and let one person feel it through your hands today.

And as this reflection closes, I think back to that chair in Pastor Chuck's office—the shame, the silence, the sentence I most needed to hear. Love lifted me up when I fell. That is the story of Christmas, and it can be the story of your day. Love moves first, and by His grace, so can you.

Prayer

Eternal Light, You descended into our darkness, clothed in humility. You loved us, not because we were worthy but because You are love. Quiet my striving and anchor me in Your grace. Shape my heart to reflect Yours—ready to serve, to give, and to love without condition. Amen.

Advent Application

Today, reflect on how God's love has reached you personally. Then respond with a purposeful act that reflects Christ's love—a word of grace, a move toward reconciliation, or a quiet sacrifice. Choose one name, one act, one time today—and let His love travel through you.

December 19

REST IN THE LOVE
THAT PURSUES YOU

*"If a man has a hundred sheep
and one of them gets lost, what will he do?
Won't he leave the ninety-nine others in the wilderness
and go to search for the one that is lost until he finds it?"*

LUKE 15:4

Next time you begin feeling like you are unnoticed and unworthy—or struggling to believe how significant your contributions are to God—remember this story: you are worth more to God than you can possibly imagine. Every individual, including you, is of immense worth to Him. If you go astray, God goes active. And nothing else matters until you're found.

— Charles R. Swindoll

Reflection

God's love rarely arrives with fanfare; it draws near and stays. I see it exemplified in my colleague Carmen. She keeps a quiet list of names for whom she prays, and when a seat is empty or a face seems weary, she notices. In morning traffic, she whispers prayers; between meetings, she listens without hurrying; when a room grows heavy, she offers a gentle word. Watching her, I recognize the Shepherd's pattern: notice who is missing, leave what is comfortable, and pursue in prayer until the one is lifted. Carmen's intercession is the quiet rhythm of God's love.

When you feel invisible, insignificant, or unsure that your life truly matters to God, remember that you are not forgotten. You are not disposable. You are deeply loved by the One who spoke light into being. He sees you. He notices when even one heart begins to wander, and He moves toward you with steadfast care.

In Luke 15, Jesus tells of a shepherd who realizes one sheep is gone. He leaves the ninety-nine and searches for the one. Logic raises questions: Why risk the many for the one? But love asks a better question: What kind of heart steps into the wilderness for a single stray? Answer: *a shepherd's heart.*

Divine love is transformational. God sees every individual; He sees a person. He sees *you.* His love doesn't wait at a distance, hoping you'll find your way back. God's love steps into the dark, calls your name, and keeps searching until you are found.

Consider the sheep. It did not wander by strategy but by small, distracted steps—chasing what seemed better until it stood alone. Isn't that how we drift? Yet the Shepherd does not scold from the hillside or shout, "Come back when you're ready." He comes to us, lifts us onto His shoulders, and rejoices.

That is the way of Christ—patient, personal, and joyful. He celebrates the return of the lost. Many have left church feeling judged rather than pursued, but the gospel moves toward people with grace. Jesus shared tables with sinners because He wanted the "lost causes" to hear good news. Before you believed in Him, God was already seeking you—and He still seeks the ones who are far off.

So the questions come to us: Have we been found by this love? Will we reflect it? Do we rejoice when others come home, or do we resent grace that stretches past our comfort? Will we, like Carmen, carry names to God and let our prayers become His pursuit?

Advent is a season of waiting, yes—but more than that, it is love breaking in. The Shepherd stepped into the wilderness for the missing one.

Jesus did the same for us. He came as a child—vulnerable, wrapped in flesh—and as the Light no darkness can extinguish. In every lonely place, in every shadow of shame or fear, the Light of Christ still seeks you today, right where you are.

You don't have to climb your way back to God. You only have to stop and listen—the footsteps of your Shepherd are already drawing near. He's not waiting for perfection; He's coming with compassion. And when He finds you, He doesn't count the miles you wandered; He carries you home with joy.

A God who forgives sinners who ask for mercy is good; a God who goes after sinners and forgives them with joy when He finds them is *astonishing*. That love sent Jesus to seek and to save the lost. *That* is the love God has for you.

To rest in God's love is to know you are pursued because you are precious. The gospel is about God finding His way to us. Advent declares: Love came looking, Love still seeks, and when He finds you, He carries you back to the fold.

So step into Christmas with open hands and a ready heart to receive His love, reflect His light, and pursue another lost sheep who needs His love—today.

Prayer

Good Shepherd, thank You for seeking me when I was far off and for never giving up on me. Help me rest in Your unwavering love today. Let that love transform how I see others—not with judgment but with joy. Amen.

Advent Application

Think of a time when you felt lost—spiritually, emotionally, or relationally—and God met you there. What did His pursuit look like? Let that memory reshape your compassion. Then choose one person who is far from God and perform one concrete act this week—call, visit, serve, or pray on the spot—not to fix this person but to offer him or her light, grace, and presence. Be the Shepherd's echo: notice, pray, go, and lift—until the one is home.

December 20

EMBRACE GOD'S CHRISTMAS MESSAGE

For this is how God loved the world:
He gave his one and only Son,
so that everyone who believes in him
will not perish but have eternal life.

JOHN 3:16

Then, with a heart weeping for His people, God dipped His brush in Calvary's scarlet ink, wrote His message on a rough wooden banner, and pinned it against an empty sky for all the world to read. Bold, crimson words: "I love you." This is the message of Christmas: Because He loves us, God has come to redeem us—to bring life and color back to our lives, to expel the darkness of our hearts.

— Charles R. Swindoll

Reflection

If Christmas tells a story, it's not one merely spoken or written; it is *lived*. Wrapped in flesh, God's love drew near—present, personal, and embodied.

I think immediately of friends like StacieNicole and Evan. They remind me of Priscilla and Aquila—always ready, always available. They lead well, but more importantly, they love well. Their smiles are authentic, their hugs heartfelt, their presence steady and reassuring. In every conversation, they listen deeply, respond intentionally, and encourage genuinely. Love like theirs describes God and *reveals* His nearness.

This is what Christmas means: the eternal Word breathed into time. It is God's everlasting declaration embodied in a Person rather than scribbled on scrolls or etched in stone. The Word became flesh. God didn't only express love; He *enfleshed* love. And that love bears a name: *Jesus*.

John 3:16 is so familiar that its shocking beauty can feel dulled by repetition. Look closely, though. In a single verse, we encounter the greatest being: *God*. The deepest motive: *love*. The most sacrificial act: *He gave His only Son*. And the widest invitation: *whoever believes*. Behind its sweeping scope lies a profoundly personal truth: *God's love speaks your name*.

What makes this love so radical is both its reach and its *source*. God moved first. He didn't wait for us to clean up our act. He didn't send terms or conditions. He gave from the depths of divine self-giving. His only Son came fully aware of the cost.

This love is active: bold, deliberate, and deeply personal. It *steps into* our pain. This love searches alleys and altars, finds the ashamed and the self-righteous, the burned-out and the broken. It is not a polite affection hoping to be noticed. It is a relentless pursuit crossing every barrier to find you.

To receive this love is to receive life, not only after death but *here* and *now*. In your waiting. In your sorrow. In your doubts and questions. This redemption isn't an abstract idea; it's a living relationship. And when the light of Christ kindles in your heart, shadows begin to retreat. This is the heart of Christmas: Christ came and *love* came—and they came *for you*.

May the warmth of that love sink deeper than seasonal sentiment. May it be your *foundation* and your *fire*. As we draw near to the Christ-child, let us walk in His light and reflect it. Let us embody His love in our speech, our service, our silence, and our sacrifice. I've seen that love close to home in StacieNicole and Evan, whose open door, steady prayers, and quiet strength turn doctrine into daily mercy.

This devotional draws to a close our journey through the Advent theme of Love. We have marveled at a love that bends low to lift us high, that sacrifices without hesitation, that shines in the darkest night, that refuses to remain far away. As we light the fourth candle, the candle of love, we arrive at the very heart of the season and lean forward in hope for the final light: the Christ candle—a flame that proclaims love is no longer an idea but a Person.

As this love burns steady within you, lift your eyes. Watch for the arrival—brilliant as sunrise, unstoppable as morning—until every shadow disappears. The Everlasting Light has stepped into the world, not in symbol or story but in flesh and blood, dwelling with us forever. This love is more than an Advent theme; it is the heartbeat of the gospel, the reason for Christmas, and the calling of our lives: to receive it, to reflect it, to carry it.

So enter Christmas as both the found and the sent. Welcome His love, shine His light, and let the arrival of Christ blaze through you until the world knows the dawn has come. Christmas is the dawn of Love arriving, the light breaking in so no night remains.

Prayer

Lord, thank You for writing Your love into history—not with ink, but with blood and grace. Thank You for loving me first, fully, and forever. Teach me to live from that love—to trust in the gift of Your Son and to mirror Your heart. Let Your love be more than a message I hear. Let it be the mission I live. Amen.

Advent Application

This week, ask: *Who around me needs to be pursued? Who needs grace in place of silence?* Take one step toward this person—write, call, forgive, invite, serve. Offer a kindness that costs—the kind of love that *echoes Christ's.*

THE BRILLIANCE OF HIS ARRIVAL

*The Light That Fills the World
in All Its Fullness*

{ December 21–25 }

We have watched hope ignite, felt peace steady our steps, and seen joy brighten the room as love warmed our souls. All of Advent has been moving toward His Arrival.

What changes when we truly believe that God has come near? I remember my first Christmas as a father. Asher was small, barely able to notice the tree, the decorations, or the music. One quiet evening, I held him in my arms and gently rocked back and forth in the soft glow of our living room. As shadows played across the walls, a single thought settled on me with surprising weight: *This is how God chose to come—close, vulnerable, dependent.* Not distant or detached. Not merely powerful, but profoundly present.

That moment reframed Advent for me. The incarnation is not a show of power but an act of intimate mercy. Christ arrived without spectacle, as a child, to remind us that God is not far away. "God is with us" (Matthew 1:23).

The Light promised is now the Light present. Christ's arrival turns long-held expectation into tangible hope, real peace, steadfast joy, and sacrificial love. Each Advent theme has been building toward this sacred moment—the arrival of Christ, the Everlasting Light, who now shines in our midst and reshapes our story.

This is the moment the horizon blushes into day. Hope has kindled, peace has steadied, joy has brightened, love has warmed— and now Christ Himself arrives, turning every promise into presence. As you light the Christ Candle and read John 1:1–14, let the room mirror the story: darkness giving way, word by word, to a growing light. In simplicity, the King has come near, and His Light is here to fill every shadow with glory.

The final candle of Advent proclaims a truth so strong history could hardly contain it: *God moved in.* This is more than the last note of a season; it is heaven and earth meeting. "The Word became flesh and made his dwelling among us" (John 1:14 NIV). The Light has come, and the world will never be the same.

Advent is about remembering that Christ came; it is about knowing that He still comes—today, in this moment. His arrival is not confined to Bethlehem or locked in the past. It is personal. Present. Persistent. Christ arrives in our fears, our doubts, our silence, and our shame—in His perfect time and meets us right where we are.

His coming—sudden, brilliant, undeniable—changes everything. After weeks of quiet longing, the Everlasting Light bursts upon the world. Shadows scatter. Silence shatters. And the themes of hope, peace, joy, and love are no longer ideas whispered in the dark—they stand before us, clothed in flesh and blood in the person of Jesus.

The word *Advent* comes from the Latin *adventus*, which translates the Greek word *parousia*, meaning "arrival" or "presence." In the New Testament it names not a date but the coming of a King. Jesus— the eternal Word—became visible Light. *He didn't only shine into the world. He made His home within it.* Heaven's quiet invasion has begun, and now, His light dwells *in us.*

This is the brilliance of the arrival: through His people, the Light keeps spreading until the earth is filled with the glory of God. So Jesus turns to us and says, *"You are the light of the world"* (Matthew 5:14). A city on a hill cannot be hidden; lamps aren't lit to be tucked away. They are lifted high so their glow reaches every corner (5:15).

So it is with you—placed not for pride but for purpose. *"Let your good deeds shine out for all to see,"* He says, *"so that everyone will praise your heavenly Father"* (5:16). The aim is the joyful exultation of God by His people.

Therefore, lift your light. In every act of love, kindness, justice, forgiveness, and integrity, let Christ's brilliance be seen. He has come. He is here. And through you, His Light keeps filling the world.

> The Light promised is now the Light present. Christ's arrival turns long-held expectation into tangible hope, real peace, steadfast joy, and sacrificial love.

Advent Wreath: Christ Candle (White)

Symbolizes the arrival of Jesus—the Light of the World

Nativity Action: Place baby Jesus in the manger.

Scripture Reading: John 1:1–14.

Reflection: As you light the Christ Candle, ask: *How will I welcome Christ's presence today?* Let the Light of the World dwell richly in you.

December 21

TRUST GOD'S PERFECT TIMING

But when the right time came, God sent his Son,
born of a woman, subject to the law.
God sent him to buy freedom for us who were slaves to the law,
so that he could adopt us as his very own children.

GALATIANS 4:4–5

Without realizing it, mighty Augustus was only an errand boy for the commencement of "the fullness of time." He was a pawn in the hand of God . . . a mere piece of lint on the pages of prophecy. While Rome was busy making history, God arrived. He pitched His fleshly tent in silence on straw . . . in a stable . . . under a star. The world didn't even notice. They overlooked Jesus the baby.

— Charles R. Swindoll

Reflection

Every December, a familiar question returns: *Why do Christians celebrate Christ's birth on December 25?*

Some trace its history to possible ties to Roman festivals like Saturnalia. Some lament how commercialization overshadows the season. These concerns rarely spring from cynicism. More often they arise from a longing for what is real—authentic worship rather than hollow habit.

Years ago, I asked Pastor Chuck how he responded to such concerns from skeptics and sincere believers alike. His response was simple and profound: "Carlos, we don't argue people into the light—we just keep turning it on."

That image endures. Jesus didn't force His way into the world. He didn't arrive with power or spectacle. But He did arrive with unshakable authority, piercing the darkness with the brilliance of divine love. As John declares, *"The Word became flesh, and dwelt among us"* (John 1:14 NASB). Whether or not Jesus was born in December, the miracle stands: He came, and His arrival was at the right time.

Paul wrote, *"When the fullness of the time came, God sent His Son"* (Galatians 4:4 NASB). The phrase, "the fullness of the time," speaks of divine choreography. The Roman Empire unified territories, laid roads, and spread a common language. Spiritually, Israel ached for deliverance; prophetically, the shadows of the Old Testament all pointed toward the Messiah. This was not coincidence. It was flawless timing.

Caesar Augustus may have issued the census thinking he was exercising imperial power. Yet behind every decree was the hand of God, guiding Joseph and Mary to Bethlehem, fulfilling Micah's prophecy (Micah 5:2). The manger was not a last resort; it was God's chosen cradle for the King of Kings.

Like then, our times feel desperate and distracting. Political corruption, economic instability, and spiritual confusion dominate headlines. None of this surprises God. His sovereignty remains unshaken. His purposes advance. His redemption weaves through every broken place.

That's why Christmas is more than a date—it's a holy reminder that *God is always right on time*. What looked like silence between Malachi and Matthew was not inactivity; it was preparation. And what we often label delay in our own stories may be God's perfect orchestration.

Christmas presses personal questions: *Will I center my life on Jesus, whatever my circumstances? Will I trust the God who timed Christ's first coming with precision to be at work in the timing of my own life?*

We chase time—calendars, deadlines, resolutions—yet God doesn't react to time; instead, He authors it. For Him, time is not pressure but providence. Every moment, whether joyful or difficult, is part of His unfolding grace.

So no, we don't worship a day. We don't cling to tradition for tradition's sake. We celebrate the Light that entered our darkness. And we keep reflecting that Light with lives that radiate His hope, peace, joy, and love.

This Christmas, stop watching the clock and start watching for grace in motion. The Light still shines—and it always arrives right on time.

Prayer

Father, You are the Lord of time, and Your timing is perfect. Thank You for sending Jesus—not a second too soon, not a moment too late. When impatience rises in the waiting, teach my heart to trust that You are at work. Help me rest in Your sovereignty. In Jesus' name, amen.

Advent Application

Where do you struggle to trust God's timing? This week, resist the impulse to rush or control outcomes. Pause and ask: *What might God be preparing in this season?* Then share a brief story with someone about a moment when God's timing proved better than your own. Let your testimony strengthen their faith and yours.

December 22

STEP INTO THE LIGHT
THAT HAS COME

*"But while I am here in the world,
I am the light of the world."*

JOHN 9:5

D o you enjoy seeing Christmas lights in your neighborhood? Have you noticed how their beauty shines most vividly in the dark? The same is true of you. You reflect Jesus—the Light of the World— most clearly when you shine for Him. Perhaps this is the season to share Christ's hope with a neighbor, volunteer at a women's shelter, or serve through your church. Embrace every opportunity to shine Christ's light into lives darkened by despair.

— Charles R. Swindoll

Reflection

Advent moves quietly, yet it carries a bold declaration: *The Light has come, and it has stepped into our darkness.* Jesus didn't wait for the world to fix itself. He entered our brokenness with purpose, with presence, and with power. His arrival was a radiant burst of grace that cut through the fog of sin and sorrow.

Jesus did more than bring light—He *is* the Light. He didn't merely point to truth; *He embodied it.* When He said, *"I am the light of the world,"* He wasn't offering a concept. He was offering *Himself*: unfiltered, undiminished, and fully divine. And tucked inside that declaration is something astonishing: one day, this Light would shine through His people.

This is more than metaphor; it is incarnation. In John 9, Jesus heals a man born blind—restoring physical sight and awakening spiritual vision. The miracle was medical and *missional.* That man's healing became a living testimony, a witness to who Jesus really is. And even now, people respond the same way: some welcome the Light, others recoil from it. Some celebrate, others resist. The tension remains, so does the Light.

The world still groans in darkness, confusion, injustice, loneliness, and fear. Yet Christ's light continues to shine, not only from heaven but through His people. Jesus made it clear when He turned to His followers and said, *"You are the light of the world"* (Matthew 5:14). This was not flattery. It was a commission. We're more than passive mirrors; we are living lamps, connected to the Source, made to radiate His presence.

That means your words matter. Your kindness matters. Your quiet presence carries eternal weight. A gentle conversation, a faithful prayer, an act of service, forgiveness when it's hardest to give—these are beams of light that pierce real darkness.

Like the man in John 9, your transformed life can spark wonder, not just about *you* but about the *One who changed you.*

Sometimes, stepping into the light begins with noticing someone. A few years ago, I was standing in line at the grocery store behind a mom who was clearly at the end of her rope—two kids fidgeting, a cart piled high, exhaustion etched across her face. She snapped at the older one, then looked down as if swallowing tears. Everything in me wanted to stay in my lane, pay, and go. Then came a quiet nudge: *Step into this.*

I touched her elbow lightly and said, "You're doing really well. I know this is a lot, but I see you." She looked up. The tears she'd been holding back finally fell. "Thank you," she whispered. "That means more than you know."

While she gathered the kids, I lifted two of the heaviest bags into her cart and steadied a third. It wasn't a speech or a solution. It was presence. And the atmosphere shifted—just a little—like a light had found a way into a crowded aisle. Her burden didn't vanish, but it felt shareable. Mine did too.

That is how the Light of Christ often moves: through nearness—through attentive love more than perfect words. The world doesn't always need our eloquence; sometimes, it simply needs us to notice, to draw near, to hold on a moment longer than expected.

Darkness is real. That's not in question. The real question is this: *will we shrink from it, or will we step into it?* Will we settle for admiring Christmas lights on houses, or will we become *living lights*—in our homes, workplaces, and friendships?

Advent offers a profound and deeply personal truth: don't only admire the lights on houses—be the lamp of God where you stand. Light travels at the speed of attention. Say, "I see you," and watch the shadows thin.

Prayer

Lord Jesus, help me shine Your light with courage and joy. Let my life reflect the hope, peace, and truth You've placed in me. Use me today to brighten someone's darkness and point him or her to You. Amen.

Advent Application

Who in your life needs the light of Christ today? Look around—your neighbor, your coworker, your child, or someone you haven't spoken to in a while? Be intentional. Let kindness speak, let presence bring peace, and let words carry hope. *Be a living light in the places that need it most.*

WELCOME THE GOD WHO DRAWS NEAR

"Look! The virgin will conceive a child!
She will give birth to a son,
and they will call him Immanuel,
which means 'God is with us.'"

MATTHEW 1:23

Christmas is about God coming down to live in this weary world with us. The long-awaited Messiah finally letting out His first cry. The Savior, the only hope for a world that drowns Him out. The conquering King of Kings, who is coming again to make wrong right once and for all. That King is OUR King! As life rages around you, please pause. Fix your eyes on Him and receive your King!

— Charles R. Swindoll

Reflection

Advent isn't merely a sentimental season filled with nostalgic songs and softly lit nativity scenes; it is far more profound and far more disruptive. At its heart lies a staggering truth: *the infinite God stepped into a fragile world.* The Creator accepted the limits of His creation. The eternal took on flesh. The invisible became touchable.

This is the miracle of *Immanuel*—God with us. He stepped into our dust—into our need, into our story.

A few years ago, I sat with a friend who had just lost someone precious. I didn't bring eloquent words or polished theology; I simply showed up. We sat in silence. It was awkward at first, then holy. After some time, he whispered through tears, *"You didn't say much. But I could feel God was here."* That is the heart of Advent: God's message is Himself—present and walking with us through everything.

Isaiah foretold that a virgin would bear a child, a sign of divine nearness (Isaiah 7:14). Centuries later, Matthew identified Jesus as the fulfillment of Isaiah's prophecy. The virgin birth stands alone in Scripture—unparalleled, mysterious, and miraculous. As the Holy Spirit breathed life into Adam from the dust, so He breathed life into Mary's womb. Jesus, the second Adam (Romans 5:12–19), came to redeem our failure and restore what was lost.

In His virgin birth, Jesus assumed true humanity without inheriting sin. Fully man and fully God. Flesh like ours, without flaw. He did not descend to lecture us; He came to live among us. "The Word became human" (John 1:14); moreover, He became acquainted with our pain, our grief, our hopes, and our brokenness. Like Pastor Chuck would say, "This is theology with skin on."

When fear closes in, *He is near*. When grief silences your voice, *He is near*. When shame whispers lies, *He is near*. When life feels too heavy to carry, yes, even then *He is near*. Christmas answers humanity's deepest ache: *"Am I alone?"* God's resounding answer remains: *"No. Never."*

So how do we respond? We can resist, like King Ahaz in Isaiah's day—clinging to control, dismissing signs, fearing change. Or we can respond like Mary, with humble surrender. Like Joseph, with obedient faith. We can welcome the God who has already come near.

Advent is a call to awaken to divine presence, not just a countdown to a holiday. The Son of God came close then. He is close now. And one day, we will see Him face to face. The miracle is not that we finally reached up to God—it is that God lovingly bent down to us. In Jesus, the God of glory entered our mess to redeem it from within.

So pause. Breathe. Rest in the truth that you are not alone. The Light has come, and He is with you—still, always, forever. Now welcome Him where you are, and live today as quiet proof that God is here.

Prayer

Immanuel, thank You for coming close. You are not a distant Savior but a present one. Teach me to trust Your nearness, to rest in Your presence, and to reflect Your light in a world still aching for hope. Amen.

Advent Application

Find a quiet moment today. Speak the name Immanuel out loud. Ask yourself: *Where do I need to feel God's nearness right now?* Write it down. Be honest. Invite Jesus into that space. Then reach out to someone who may need the same reminder. Let your presence speak of His presence.

December 24

JOIN HEAVEN'S CHORUS OF GLORY

"Glory to God in highest heaven,
and peace on earth to those with whom God is pleased."

LUKE 2:14

Jesus was wrapped in mystery. True "awe" resides in the mystery of Jesus' nature. Even in this tiny baby, we find undiminished deity clothed in perfect humanity. Linking two natures together in one personality, housed in one unique body—the God-man Jesus was born. That's awe-inspiring mystery! No wonder hosts of angels declared in unison, "Glory to God in highest heaven!" (Luke 2:14). What words fail to describe, only worship can express.

— Charles R. Swindoll

Reflection

The world had its eyes fixed on emperors and empires. Power lived in palaces. Caesar Augustus, cloaked in titles and tribute, was called the "prince of peace." Yet heaven announced another King—cradled, not crowned; welcomed by shepherds, not guarded by soldiers.

Then, on a quiet hillside outside Bethlehem, glory split the silence. The sky swelled with worship. Angels filled the night with a thunderous song for Christ alone. *"Glory to God in the highest, / And on earth peace among people with whom He is pleased"* (Luke 2:14 NASB). This was not a heartwarming carol. It was a cosmic announcement—a proclamation that the glory of God, once veiled behind temple curtains, now wrapped itself in a newborn's cry. Light had arrived, and nothing would be the same.

In Luke 2:14, the angels proclaim two divine realities that always go hand-in-hand: *God's glory* and *humanity's peace*. This is not peace forged by treaties or distraction; it is peace through presence— peace born in a Person. Then comes a phrase that might give us pause: *". . . to those with whom God is pleased."* Who are they? The faithful ones, as Scripture declares, *"It is impossible to please God without faith"* (Hebrews 11:6).

God's favor doesn't rest on the proud or the polished. It rests on the trusting. Those who stop striving and begin to surrender. Like Mary and Joseph, they receive God's Word with humble obedience. That is the heart of Christmas: *faith expressed as welcoming presence.*

I think of Christmas Eve in my hometown in Mexico. The aroma of tamales filled the air as our whole family—believers and not-so-devout—gathered to celebrate. We'd walk together through the neighborhood during the *posada*, an annual feast reenacting Mary and Joseph's search for shelter. Candles glowed in the night. Voices rose in song. And at last, a door would open with the welcoming words: "Come in, holy pilgrims!"

We'd enter the house, break the piñata, share laughter, and prepare for the moment we'd all been waiting for—gently placing baby Jesus in the manger. Not everyone in my family claimed deep faith, but there was always a sense of reverence that stilled us, even if just for a moment. Because on that night, something sacred brushed against our ordinary lives. Christians and skeptics stood side by side, drawn into the beauty of the story: *God came near.*

It wasn't about having perfect theology; it was about presence— God with us. Right there, woven into music, food, and family, heaven drew close.

The angels on that first Christmas Eve didn't sing for their own joy alone. They invited the shepherds—and us—into their joy. That chorus still rises. The invitation still stands. Will you join it?

Tonight, don't just admire the song—sing it. Let your next word, your next decision, your next act of love echo heaven's anthem. Let your life say what your lips sometimes forget to speak: *"Glory to God in the highest,"* and become His vessel of peace where the world aches most. Glorify God where you stand—then carry His peace wherever you step.

Prayer

Eternal Light, open my eyes to Your glory and soften my heart to Your peace. Let my life rise like a song of praise. As the angels sang of Your greatness, may I reflect it—not just with words, but with how I live. Amen.

Advent Application

Pause and slow the day. Choose one decision you'll make today—just one—and ask: *How can this glorify God?* Then do it: a kind word, a forgiving choice, a quiet act of generosity. Let worship move beyond carols and take shape in action. Join the chorus.

December 25

WALK DAILY IN EVERLASTING LIGHT

Your sun will never set;
your moon will not go down.
For the LORD will be your everlasting light.
Your days of mourning will come to an end.

ISAIAH 60:20

On a rescue mission designed by His Father before time began, Jesus silently slipped into our world, breathed our air, felt our pain, became acquainted with our sorrows, suffered and died for our sins . . . to show us the way out of our darkness and into His glorious light. This Christmas, may you know the warmth of the Savior's love spreading over you. May the beauty of the season remind you of His intense concern for every detail of your life and His great, sacrificial love for you.

— Charles R. Swindoll

Reflection

It's *Christmas Day!* The house wakes early, children tumble out of bed, and the air crackles with laughter—paper flying, names called, hearts full. But even with all the excitement, today is more than a calendar date. Today signals the beginning of an eternal chapter: the arrival of Light that never dims.

In our home, we keep a simple tradition. Karla and I stay in our pajamas, settle near the Christmas tree, and let our son, Asher, assume his honored post as "present-passer-outer." He takes the job seriously—and his true delight is volunteering to help open everyone else's gifts with the unrestrained energy of a wrapping-paper whirlwind.

And of course, there's Snoopy—Asher's loyal stuffed companion—wearing a tiny sombrero and shaking maracas to the rhythm of José Feliciano's *"Feliz Navidad"* on repeat. It plays so often that by sundown no one in our house can forget what we're celebrating.

And then we pause. Coffee in hand, gratitude in our chests, we remind Asher—and ourselves—that the greatest gift never sat under a tree. He arrived wrapped in swaddling clothes, sent by the Father: *Jesus, God with us.*

That moment steadies the day. Christmas is not only a memory; it is promise—promise kept in Bethlehem and promise still unfolding in glory.

I remember Pastor Chuck saying during a Christmas Eve service, "Every nativity scene we set up is a declaration: He came once. He's coming again." The story reaches beyond the manger. The horizon still hums with His promise—the second coming many expected the first time. This coming will be public and glorious: the arrival of the King who will reign in justice and peace.

Yet heaven saw our deepest need. Before we needed a Sovereign to rule, we needed a Savior to redeem. So He came first in humility—Lamb before Lion—to live the life we could not live and die the death we could not bear, rescuing now and returning one day to restore. In that holy arc, the cradle points to the cross, and the cross guarantees the crown.

All through Scripture, darkness rarely wears a friendly face. Egypt felt a darkness you could touch. The poor and fatherless are pictured as walking in the shadows. Sinai's cloud hid the Holy One. John writes it plain: *"God is light, and there is no darkness in him at all"* (1 John 1:5). No wonder our hearts long for morning. Isaiah promises a day when lamps and lunar phases step aside because the Lord Himself will be our Everlasting Light. Genesis called day and night "good," but those good lights were signposts pointing to the better Light, the Son, who ends the night so His people never stumble again.

Light is a moral word as much as a visible one. It speaks of God's blazing purity—a brightness only the cleansed can endure. The prophets foresaw a washed people ready to live in that light. In Christ, that cleansing is complete; now we await the full sunrise when every shadow finally flees. When Isaiah spoke of a light that would never fade (Isaiah 9:2; 60:19–20), he was announcing reality. Christ is that Everlasting Light. The seasonal glow of Christmas dims when the tree is boxed and the music quiets, but Jesus keeps shining—through grief and questions, through celebrations and callings. So lift your eyes and step forward: *The Light has risen, and He will not set!*

So hear the good news fresh on this morning: the Light has not merely come to us; He now shines through us. Christmas is a commissioning. You carry His Light into boardrooms and break rooms, kitchen tables and hospital beds, sidewalks and sanctuary aisles. Wherever you go, the Light goes with you.

And now, as the final act of Advent, light the Christ Candle—the center flame, the source of every other light. If possible, dim the room so the brightness grows as the candle glows. Gather your family, or sit quietly alone, and read John 1:1–14 aloud. Let the words rise like dawn:

The Word gave life to everything that was created,
and his life brought light to everyone. . . .
So the Word became human and made his home among us.
(John 1:4, 14)

Let this day be more than sweet; let it be sacred. Let it send you. The same Light who lay in a manger now lives in your heart—and He walks with you into every tomorrow.

As we close this Advent journey, don't place a period at the end of the poem. Think of today as the comma before eternity's next verse. We have followed the glow of hope, peace, joy, and love—each ray leading us to Jesus: the Light who came, the Light who stays, the Light who will come again.

This Light isn't confined to sanctuaries or seasons. He slips quietly into laundry rooms and late-night conversations, long commutes and crowded kitchens. So as the candles flicker low and the tamales begin to cool, remember: His Light still burns brightly—because He lives in you. And where His Light shines through you, darkness does not get the last word.

The Light has come—so rise and carry Him into the ordinary until every shadow bows to His dawn.

¡Feliz Navidad, de todo corazón!

Merry Christmas with all my heart!

Prayer

Everlasting Light, thank You for entering our world with unshakable love. On this Christmas Day, I celebrate not just Your birth but Your presence in every part of my life. Illuminate my heart. Lead my steps. Help me reflect Your joy, hope, peace, and love—today and always. Amen.

Advent Application

Today is not the finish line; it is the starting bell. In a quiet moment, name one place in your life still waiting for God's Light and welcome Him there. Then ask, *Who near me needs that same Light?* Reach out to him or her. Offer love, prayer, or simply show up. Before bedtime, share one sentence of praise with someone: *"The Light has come—and He is with us."* Walk daily in His everlasting Light, and let the world see the glow.

You are bearers of the Light. Step into January with practices that keep the flame lit: Word, prayer, table, neighbor.

CONCLUSION

As we come to the end of this sacred Advent journey, remember: the truths we've embraced are year-long. Hope, peace, joy, and love are eternal realities, rooted in the person of Jesus Christ, our Everlasting Light.

We have moved from a first glimmer to a brilliant arrival. What began as promise now stands as presence: Christ's light fills the world—and, by grace, our lives—with His fullness.

The prophet Isaiah declared:

> *"Your sun will never set;*
> *your moon will not go down.*
> *For the LORD will be your everlasting light.*
> *Your days of mourning will come to an end."* (Isaiah 60:20)

Jesus fulfills that promise. He shines into the hidden and hurting places all year long. His light is the heartbeat of redemption.

I think of my son Asher's simple wisdom: *"Without lights, there wouldn't be Christmas."* In a deeper sense, he is right. Jesus is the Light who breaks every shadow—*"the true Light, that gives light to everyone"* (John 1:9 NIV).

That Light is the same Light that Simeon cradled when he spoke:

> *"A light to reveal God to the nations,*
> *and he is the glory of your people Israel!"* (Luke 2:32)

The same light that hovered over the fields of Bethlehem now *lives within us.*

As these pages close, lift your gaze. Fix your eyes on Christ—your Savior, your Redeemer, your King. Let your life glow with His unmistakable light.

> *In Him was life, and the life was the Light of mankind. And the Light shines in the darkness, and the darkness did not grasp it.* (John 1:4–5 NASB)

May the Everlasting Light shine in you and through you—today, tomorrow, and always.

EPILOGUE
From Promise to Presence:
Now What?

As the last carols fade and the ornaments rest in their boxes, remember: Christmas is a doorway into what comes next. The candles that once trembled with anticipation may be extinguished, but the Light they proclaimed still burns undiminished. Christ, our Everlasting Light, goes with us—steady and sure—into the holy ordinary of our days.

We have traced the *Cycle of Light*: hope kindling, peace settling, joy rising, love warming, arrival blazing. Now, the call is simple and strong: embody what you have received. Choose faithfulness over perfection; choose presence that lingers and listens. In Christ, the common becomes a chapel, and the daily becomes an altar.

So we live as people lit from within. In a world clouded by fatigue and fear, we do not outshout the darkness; we outshine it. Offer a word at the right moment. Lend a listening ear when answers run thin. Whisper a prayer for someone who may never know your name. Small in human eyes—yet sparks that travel further than we imagine.

Let the humility of Jesus temper your words and the wisdom of Jesus guide your decisions. Make room at your table—and margin in your schedule—for the weary, the overlooked, the searching. Be a lamp on a stand in family and friendship, at work and in your neighborhood, even in the unnoticed corners of your digital life—creating spaces where others encounter the living presence of Christ.

When the road feels long, return to the Light: hope that anchors, peace that steadies, joy that strengthens, love that gives itself away. Seek His guidance for the next faithful step. Leave the years in His hands. Let Scripture be your lamp, prayer your breath, and obedience your quiet yes in the small places where heaven's work is done on earth.

Ultimately, the charge is clear: *be a vessel of His Light.* Carry the essence of Christmas into classrooms and kitchen tables, into meetings and margins, onto screens and sidewalks. Let His love lead you. Let His truth hold you. Let His light be seen through you wherever He has placed you.

Lift the light you've been given. Someone's night is waiting for His dawn.

ABOUT THE AUTHOR

Carlos A. Zazueta serves as the lead pastor of Insight for Living in Spanish and is the voice behind *Visión Para Vivir*, one of IFL's international broadcasts. For nearly two decades, he has ministered alongside Pastor Charles R. Swindoll—one of the most trusted and beloved voices in Christian teaching—helping proclaim biblical truth to Spanish-speaking audiences around the world.

Born in Culiacán, Sinaloa, México, Carlos pursued his theological and pastoral training in the United States. He holds both a master of theology (ThM) and a doctor of ministry (DMin) from Dallas Theological Seminary. His bilingual and bicultural background brings a rich, nuanced perspective to Christian discipleship, allowing him to bridge cultures with clarity, compassion, and conviction.

Through preaching, teaching, broadcasting, and writing, Carlos serves the global church with a heart anchored in Scripture and a deep desire to help others see Jesus more clearly and follow Him more fully. His messages combine theological depth, pastoral warmth, and practical wisdom—a rare blend that resonates powerfully across generations and cultures.

Carlos lives in Texas, with his wife, Karla—"the calm in their family storm"—and their son, Asher—"the storm." Their home is a joyful blend of introverted peace and extroverted energy, often filled with laughter, music, and a sincere love for Jesus. Whether enjoying a quiet evening or breaking into an impromptu living room dance party, their family holds fast to one unshakable truth: even in the chaos, *Christ's light still shines.*